I0749575

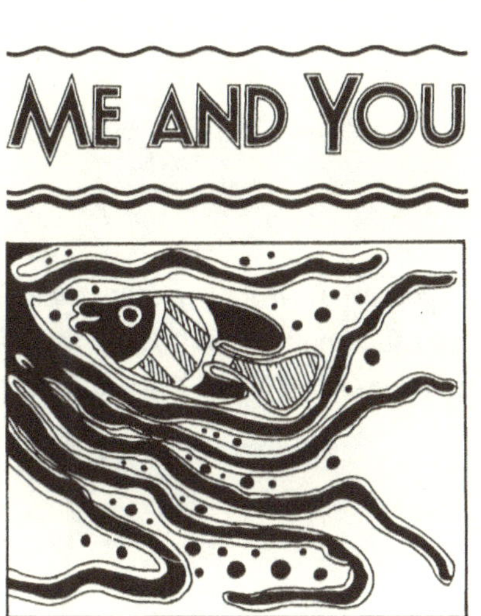
ME AND YOU

Whether you are a white person or a black person, caring and sharing is what it is all about—me and you together—and that's the beauty part of it.

Della Walker, 1989

ME AND YOU

The life story of Della Walker

as told to Tina Coutts

ABORIGINAL STUDIES PRESS

First published in 1989
by Aboriginal Studies Press
Reprinted 2020, 2021, 2026

Aboriginal and Torres Strait Islander people are respectfully advised that this publication contains names and images of deceased persons and culturally sensitive information.

Aboriginal Studies Press is the publishing arm of the Australian Institute of Aboriginal and Torres Strait Islander Studies.

PO Box 553, Canberra, ACT 2601
Phone: (61 2) 6246 1183
Fax: (61 2) 6261 4288
Email: asp@aiatsis.gov.au
Web: www.aiatsis.gov.au/asp/about.html

National Library of Australia Cataloguing-in-Publication data:
Walker, Della, 1932–2004
Me and you: the life story of Della Walker as told to Tina Coutts
ISBN 978 0 85575 212 5
1 Walker, Della [2] Aborigines, Australian–New South Wales Women–Biography [3] Aborigines, Australian–New South Wales–Social life and customs I Coutts, Tina, 1955– II Australian Institute of Aboriginal Studies III Title
994 40049915

Designed by Maureen MacKenzie, Aboriginal Studies Press
Typeset in ITC Stone Informal by Aboriginal Studies Press
Illustrations and maps by Tryphena McShane and Lewis Walker
Photographic research by Caroline Pascoe
Cover by Carolyn Brooks, Media Graphics, incorporating line drawings by Tryphena McShane

Contents

Foreword

In 1985, I was employed on a project for the National Library of Australia, researching the cultural context of unemployment among women. This involved recording and transcribing the life stories of women from all walks of life. One of the things that stood out above all others was that the most ordinary of women had the most extraordinary experiences to relate. Della Walker was one of these women who freely and openly shared her experiences. She was very willing to talk with us, something which is indeed rare among rural Aboriginal women. She also expressed genuine concern regarding unemployment and the implications it had for her people.

Having done brief oral history recordings of her life for the National Library's project, I discovered what a wealth of knowledge Della had to share. We discussed her desire to write a book, which previously had seemed an impossibility until she heard how much of her life had been captured on the tapes. Della realised that with the added help of a tape recorder, I could become the pen in her hand.

Then Della, Tryphena McShane, Caroline Pascoe and myself further refined the concept of the book and planned how we could go about it. We were all enthusiastic and knew that we four women could work together to produce it. Three daunting years later, *Me and You* is a reality—a reality of which we are proud because we were black and white women working together in harmony.

During these years, Della proved to be a natural storyteller who provided living images of what she wanted to share. Nevertheless, there were many episodes in her life which she was reluctant to tell, and others which were recalled with great difficulty. Della was forever mindful about not offending anyone, living or dead, so there are some gaps in her story. Her overriding concern for the future of her culture, however, made her determined to put her story in print because she believes it to be a viable avenue to help retain Aboriginal heritage for future generations. *Me and You* is of interest, not solely because of Della's Aboriginality, but also because she is a woman—a woman of strong convictions.

Having decided to go ahead with the writing of this book, we talked about the structure and selected the experiences we would concentrate on. There were some sixteen hours of recording to be transcribed. The original recordings and transcriptions are lodged with the Oral History Section of the National Library of Australia. There was also additional research to be done in the form of 'casual' conversations with people who knew Della. This was extremely time-consuming and involved a lot of travelling.

Della wished that her Aboriginal English be transformed into Standard English. I felt reluctant to do this as I believed that some of the uniqueness of her story would be lost. However, I can now see that she was right. Editing was required where details were repetitious or where the tenses were ambiguous or incorrect, and grammatical structures were also changed, but only where essential to enable clear expression of Della's thoughts and to avoid confusion. Additional links between the chapters also had to be written and some episodes were transposed so that similar experiences appeared together. Punctuation was a problem, so we adopted a simple and conservative approach of short sentences or the use of commas in strings of phrases. Otherwise, Della's story has been left intact and I believe her sense of rhythm in storytelling and her unique way of expression have been retained. It is also true, as with any reminiscences, that thoughts of early experiences bring later ones to mind but the book is basically chronological in its structure, although there are occasional cross-references to later events.

Originally it was intended to use excerpts from the interviews with other people interspersed throughout the book so that readers might gain some further insight into Della's personality. Deciding who would be included was difficult because Della has so many friends and has the ability to bring out the best in almost everyone she meets. We settled on using the reminiscences of just five people from both her childhood and from the latter part of her life: Desi Ferguson, Doreen Castle, Adelaide and John Laurie and Maggie Olesen They were happy to share their experiences with us. It is significant that these people who are included in her book are both Aboriginal and non-Aboriginal. This was purely coincidental, but exemplifies Della's philosophy and indeed the theme of her book, *Me and You.*

To check the spellings of Aboriginal words, we consulted *Geytenbeck: A Gidabal Grammar* from the Australian Institute of Aboriginal Studies, *Aboriginal Studies Resource Book* from the Bonalbo High School, *Australian Dreaming* by Jennifer Isaacs and published by Lansdowne Press, and several booklets by Margaret Sharpe published by the Institute for Aboriginal Community Development and the Northern Rivers College of Advanced Education. Where there has been any discrepancy we sought the opinion of local Aboriginal people and have given their opinions precedence.

In transcribing *Me and You,* I hope I have done Della and her family justice. I thank her for her love and patience and for allowing me to become part of her special family. I would also like to thank my children, Carmen and Jessi. They have had to put up with a busy mum who perhaps hasn't had as much time to be with them as she would like. For their patience, pride, understanding and involvement in Della's project, I thank them. I would also like to thank the staff of Aboriginal Studies Press who offered constructive criticism and assistance in the editing, design and production of this book.

Della has now returned to her roots in Maclean, she has turned a full circle. Her wish to become an ordained pastor has been realised, along with her desire to be a counsellor in the prison system. She has organised a new dance troupe and is available anytime as a consultative person within the community. She is also writing down the Yaegl language for use in the local schools.

Me and You takes the reader from the innocent laughter of childhood through to the joys and sorrows of adulthood. It tells of the incorporation of Della's heritage into her daily life via such mediums as language, diet, love of the land, kinship and mission days. Her enthusiasm for what life has to offer is an inspiration to others. The book also tells of Della's deep trust in the Lord, and how her faith supported her during her own personal tragedies.

Della's book is a reflection of her pride in her Aboriginality. She is not taking a political stance nor is she seeking sympathy. She is sharing her experiences, both traditional and contemporary, so that future generations of Aboriginal children will not be condemned for the colour of their skin. For one of the most important aspects of Della's message is the need for relationships between 'me and you' (black and white) to be fostered and nurtured. Her life and her book show us how this is possible.

Tina Coutts
Tabulam 1989

Acknowledgements

I feel there is a great need for bridges between our cultures so that God's love can flow between 'me and you'. It is hoped that this book can help bridge the gap. I have been fortunate enough to have the help and support of three very special women.

Firstly I would like to thank Tina Coutts for putting so much time and effort into the recording and writing of my life story. I believe she has a special understanding of my people and without her encouragement and support this book would not have been written. I would like to thank Tryphena McShane for her beautiful illustrations and her ability to draw through my Aboriginal eyes. Thanks also to Caroline Pascoe for her work on the photographs. I believe she has captured the true spirit of our people.

Many others have helped with this book. I am proud of and thank my son Lewis for his drawings of our dreamtime. Special thanks to Desi Ferguson, Adelaide and my late brother John Laurie, Doreen Castle and Maggie Olesen for allowing their thoughts and memories to be used.

Photographs were kindly supplied by Austin Soorley, Brenda Smith, Susan Donnelly, Mrs K Bolton, the Maclean Historical Society, the Yamba Historical Society and the Grafton *Daily Examiner.* To these people and organisations, thank you.

Many organisations provided support. I thank the National Library of Australia for the loan of recording and transcribing equipment, the Tabulam Primary and Tabulam Pre-school for use of the phone and photocopier, and the Aboriginal Arts Board for financial assistance.

There are many individuals who helped with research. I cannot name everyone for there are too many, but they know who they are and I thank them all.

Finally, I wish to thank my family—my daughters, my sons, my grandchildren and the many others who call me 'Ma Walker'—they have all done me proud.

Map of the mouth of the Clarence River showing Ulgundahi Island and Yamba. Drawn by Tryphena McShane.

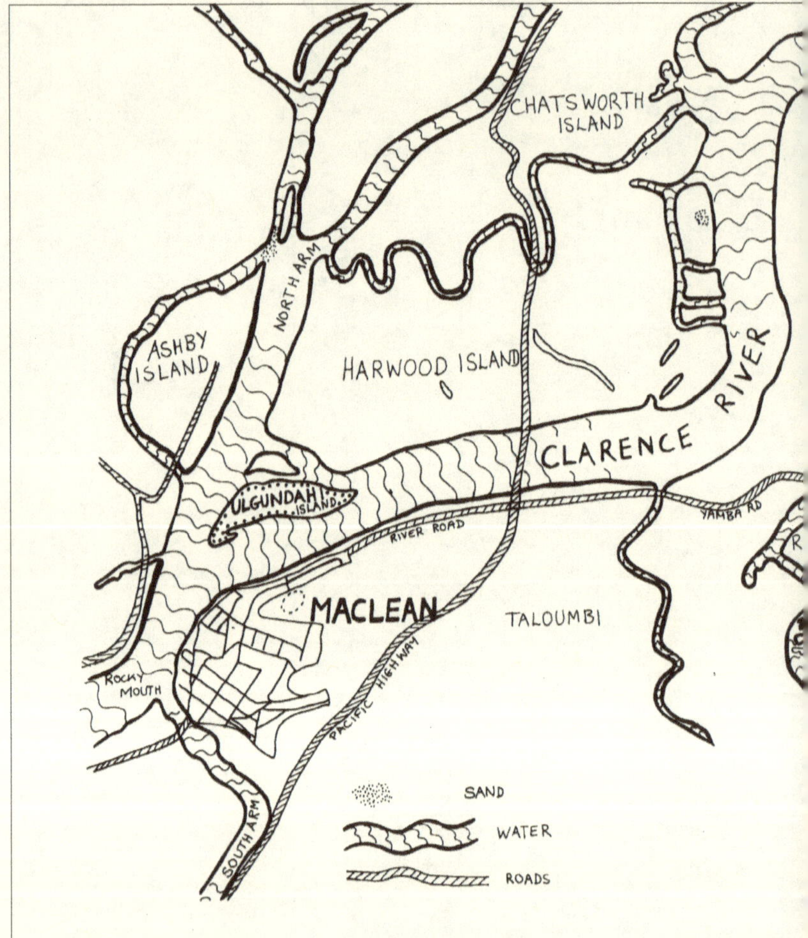

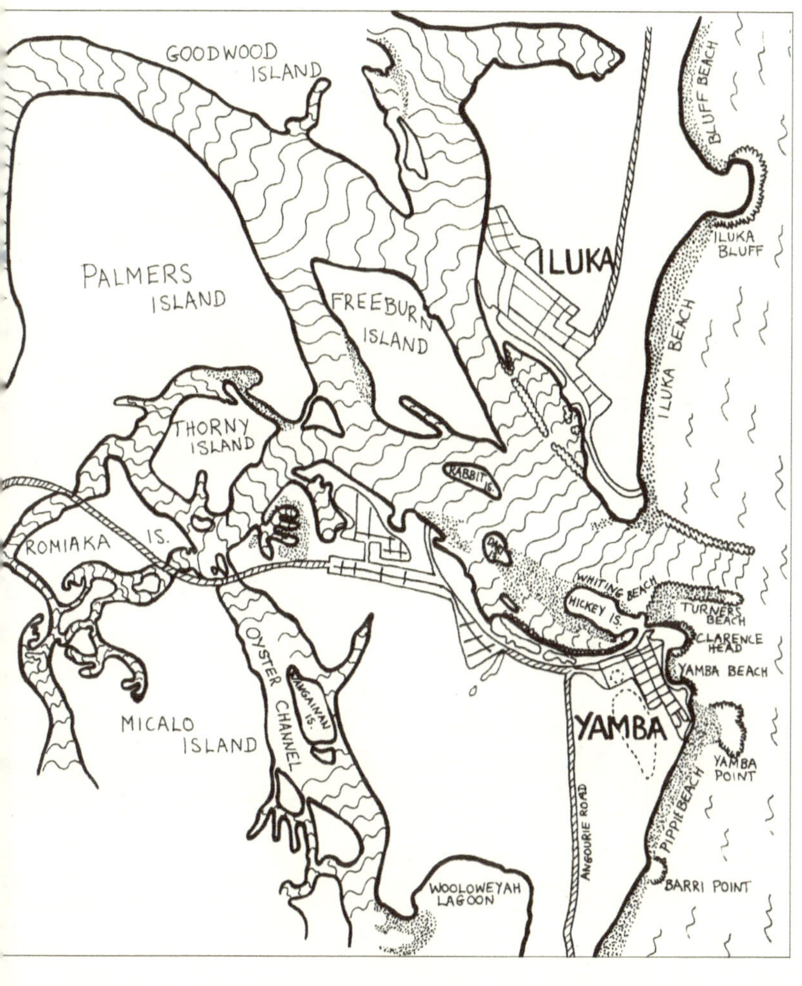
GOODWOOD
ISLAND
PALMERS
ISLAND
FREEBURN
ISLAND
ILUKA
BLUFF BEACH
ILUKA
BLUFF
ILUKA BEACH
THORNY
ISLAND
RABBIT IS.
DART IS.
ROMIAKA IS.
WHITING BEACH
HICKEY IS.
TURNERS
BEACH
CLARENCE
HEAD
YAMBA BEACH
OYSTER CHANNEL
YANGAINAN IS.
MICALO
ISLAND
YAMBA
YAMBA
POINT
PIPPIE BEACH
ANGOURIE ROAD
BARRI POINT
WOOLOWEYAH
LAGOON

Recollections by Desi Ferguson

Della came and lived with us for a while at Coffs Harbour. We were only little bits of kids. We had this pet possum called Rex. The kids slept in one bed with Della in the middle. This possum would come out at night and it got real savage. If you moved any part of your body the possum would grab it. No matter what part you moved—your head, arm, ankle or foot—it would grab it. So one night we were laying there as large as life and Della said to her brother Alan, 'Have a look. See where the possum is.' We couldn't feel it crawling on the bed because we had a big eiderdown on top of us. So Alan, he pulled the eiderdown over his eyes and looked around the bed. The possum was sitting at the top of the bed and it dived down and bit a big chunk out of his head, blood everywhere. Della started screaming, then we all started screaming. My father hunted it back with a stick then. It was a pet, raised it from a little one. We thought it was a boy but it became pregnant and savage.

One day we took Della out hunting. While we were hunting we saw this koala bear running across the paddock. We thought it was a monkey and we chased it. We got some sticks to bash it and while we were bashing it, the koala bear was crying its eyes out. While it was crying, Della was crying as well. She said, 'Don't be cruel. Let the poor monkey live.' Well, never seen a koala bear up close, not even a picture of one. We didn't know, so we killed it and took it home. We were going to eat it but Della wouldn't touch it. She said, 'Youse are cruel killing that poor animal.'

Very soft-hearted she was. But oh, when she got a temper up she really let fly, didn't think twice what was going to happen to her. She just stepped into a row, especially between the brothers. Oh! She was very quick-tempered, not a bad temper. Only lasted for a very short period then it was all over, just a couple of minutes and it was gone. I remember the time when Della was only a girl, down there at Yamba, and the brothers got into a fight. Her brother, Billo, chucked the horrors and grabbed an axe. He was gonna cut everybody up. Della ran from nowhere and Billo made a chop at her leg, so of course she jumped the axe. As she jumped, she just let Billo have it with her right hand. Flattened him, knocked him as cold as a maggot.

When we were kids at Yamba, we used to have mud-stick fights. The girls used to get the springy branches off the paperbark trees and put a bit of clay on them. We'd shoot the mud off, they really stung. All us black kids here at the mission used to fight all the white kids in town. The white kids had pop guns and shanghais and all we had were our mud-sticks. We used to flog them every time. Della was a ring leader but they were just two-bit squabbles and that was it, used to be over, finished with.

Sometimes we'd walk way out the back of Angourie and Shelley, getting Christmas Bells and Boronias. We'd sell them so we could go to the pictures. We also used to make sand bottles. We'd get clear bottles and put all different coloured sands in them. Della was pretty good at drawing designs in bottles. We used to draw sailing boats and things like that. You'd have to put the colours in all the right places. It would take about a month to get the different sands. We'd make designs with a piece of wire and sell them for three or four dollars—it was quids in those days. That gave us pocket money to go the pictures.

Other times when we were out at Shaw's Drive we'd play marbles with pearls. Used to go diving for them, get a pocket full of pearls and start the biggest game of marbles. To us they were only marbles. Whoever won the marbles at the end of the day would use them in shanghais to knock down birds. We knew there were plenty of pearls there to get. We didn't realise they were valuable.

We were only blacks. No-one would take any notice of us. We were treated like dogs but we learned to accept it. Today it's a different story. Della never had any ill-feeling towards the white people because she got on with them. She enjoyed their company. See we were all kids and we grew up with them, so we had no complaints, we were all happy. It was mainly the parents who had a hard time. When we played sports, Della was their idol, all the Lauries were. They were so well liked by everybody. There was no segregation. It was really good.

The Laurie family were all very well respected because of the old man. He was a real champion. He was Della's father, old Rocky. I don't think anyone saw the mother because she stayed home all the time. She never went anywhere. The old bloke was a real sportsman and I think Della got it from him, Della and her sister Lillian. Lillian was a good sportswoman. Old Rocky, he got on with everybody, same as Della. If there was work to do, Rocky would do it. That's where the kids got it from, they all worked. The mother worked all the time too but no-one would ever see her because she was always in the background. Rocky held the limelight. That's how it was, she accepted it and so did the family.

See the kids today they've got everything. We had nothing but everything. We used to all swim in the raw when we were up on the island. We just had no swimmers. There were sharks but there was never any mention of them. We never even thought about it. Nobody was ever taken. Most of the girls on the island were young teenagers. They still swam in the nude, it wasn't indecent. It was so hot you went straight in, even the men and women.

Moving off the island, I think it was a case of follow the leader—where old Rocky went everyone else went. He decided to come to Yamba to live and the Randalls (that's his wife's relations), moved over to Maclean. I think we ended up with the better end of the stick though. Rocky had a couple of relations already living here and I think he moved down to be near them. Only little tin huts they were. We found there was more to be done down at Yamba, foodwise. We didn't have to go far for food.

Old Rocky made himself a couple of fishing rods and he'd feed the family. There were some big fish around then but they've all gone because of the trawlers. He must have caught a world record snapper. We were staying out at Shelley Beach. There was myself and my family and Della's brother, Alan. I don't know if Della was with us. Anyway, Rocky came back at daylight one morning just on sun up. We could see this thing shining on his back. It was the biggest snapper. He had it by the gills over his head and it was dragging along the ground. He got no recognition. If you caught one like that today, you'd be a celebrity. He just caught it to feed us.

My mother was Della's sister, Margaret. She was the eldest in the family and that's why Della's not much older than I am. What I can recall of Della as a young teenager, well we got on exceptionally well with everyone. I've never seen her do anything in anger. She just didn't like anyone drinking but she accepted it because she couldn't tell her elders what to do—her brothers mainly.

She worked as a kid down at the Craigmore Guest House. Nearly all the black girls around here used to work at the Craigmore. They were the only ones that'd give the blacks a go. They found them to be very clean and whenever the girls were asked to do something they never hesitated or whinged about it, they just did it.

She also worked for the Teeces. They were good to everybody—the old Teece family. They were just so old-fashioned. They had a butcher shop and when they said you'd get fresh meat, they meant fresh. It was killed in the morning and you got it that afternoon. None of this killing it and leaving it for a while. They killed it and they ate it. They had their own slaughter shed out the back of the industrial area. We'd go out there and get all the stomachs, tripe and livers to eat. Mr Teece used to give it to us. We survived, we managed. We had some fantastic times as kids. We never slung off what colour we were, we didn't and they didn't.

Della moved to Tabulam and married Willie and started her own family, her family today. I still don't know them all, she's got that many of them. I talk to the kids today and they ask me how I'm going. Well I've got to figure out who I'm talking to. Della, she comes and goes. Della's that used to having a tribe around her. I'm the opposite. The less I see of my mob, the better I like it. I don't mind them visiting once a month or something, but any more is just too much for me and the missus.

I look at Della and Lillian and they seem to have the same outlook on life—free and easy. The more they have around them, the more they seem to like it. I said to them, 'I don't know how you do it.' I couldn't do it. I've never classified Della as an aunty, she's more like a sister. It's just a feeling I've got. I don't call her 'Aunty' now. Della's a very loving mother, a very considerate woman, a very sociable woman. She'll go out of her way to help in any way she can. She's a bit crazy too. She's crazy to herself, her own health, ignores her own health to help others. She is not a well person, but you can't tell her. She's too busy helping others, though she thrives on it.

Life on the island

I want to tell you about my people so that you can come to know and understand us as Aboriginal people. I was born in 1932 on Ulgundahi Island, not far from where the Clarence River meets the sea. It was there that I spent my school days. We used to go hunting and fishing, and we helped the fishermen with the nets. It was there that we grew up—all together with my family—my brothers, my sisters, my Mum and Dad. We had a lovely time on the island as I can remember.

Whiting

I remember my Uncle Claudie who used to plant vegetables and also he had cane growing. Everyone of those people, my uncles who lived there, they'd all come to help one another to cut the cane. They worked together side-by-side, used to carry the cane in their arms and fill the punts that way. They had no derricks. They had nothing on that island but they did it themselves. They were very hard-working men, always helping one another, sharing. We used to share with one another. If we didn't have something we would go and ask our aunty and she'd share with us. My Mum and Dad struggled to support us. We got rations but it wasn't enough for us. When we came home after school we'd row over to the mainland to our help Mum and Dad pick potatoes, peas and beans. We were always there to help, and we were very proud of ourselves for doing that, helping our Mum and Dad.

One year a great big flood came over the island. We had to move to the mainland. We were there for three months and didn't go to school, but we used to go hunting every day in the bush—honey, porcupine, possum, goanna, kangaroo. We would chase them, throw stones at them and run them down, then take what we caught in the bush back to our Mum and Dad so we could have our meals. We just loved doing it because it was so much fun. It was hard but it was fun. Dad and Mum worked very hard to keep us. Being a family of eight girls and six boys it was hard, even to clothe us, but we would help our Mum do the work. I loved my mother and father very much, we all did.

When the floods came over the island I'd stay with my grandmother at Ashby, on the mainland. I was always with her. She wasn't far away from Mum and Dad. My grandmother had a little place of her own, a little hut and I would sleep in that hut with her. She used to always tell us stories. Some stories she told us I just can't remember but this is a special one I would like to share with you. The story is 'the waratah and the pool of tears' and is about a pretty girl and a handsome young man. The Gumbaigl people came from Kempsey and the Yaegl people from Yamba and Maclean. They met halfway for the battle in this story, at a place between Grafton and Baryulgil. The red waratah tree grows from the rock and the waterfall flows beneath it. These stories that my grandmother told me mean a lot to me because now I can pass them on to my own grandchildren and keep our Aboriginal culture strong.

The Gongan (girl) and the Birrigan (young man) were in love. They spent many hours walking on the rocks together. One day the Birrigan told her he had to go and fight in a battle. The Gumbaigl and Yaegl people were going to have a battle and the Birrigan had to go. The Gongan didn't want him to go but he had to go with the elders. He had no choice. He told her to sit on a rock and wait for him to come back.

While the Gongan waited she made a cloak of red feathers and put it around her shoulders to keep warm and so the Birrigan would be able to see her from a long way away when he came back. There was only one person left after the battle, an old man, who came to the Gongan as an eagle. He saw her sitting there and told her that the Birrigan was killed in the battle with a *bilar* (spear).

Night after night she sat there and she cried and she cried and she cried. Eventually her tears turned into a waterfall from the rock she was sitting on. She was there so long that her family came to look for her. They found a red waratah tree where she had been sitting on the rock. She had turned into that red waratah tree and they reckon that tree is still there.

Anyway, after the flood we moved back to Ulgundahi Island. We went to school there. The teacher's name was Alan Cameron. He was a nice old teacher but I didn't learn very much at that age. All the same it was still mixing and growing with the rest of the family. I enjoyed life and I still enjoy life today. It was lovely on the island back in those days.

When we finished up after school there would be fishermen who would come over from the main town and put out nets. We used to swim not far away and watch them. When it was time to pull the nets in we would always be there to help them. One lot on one side and one lot on the other side, pulling the net in. We'd get all the undersized fish and we'd take them home to our mother and father. We just used to love doing it because it was part of us.

We used to work together. We used to share together and that's the beauty part of it, sharing, giving. This is how we used to live on the island—helping one another. Every family had two and a half acres to grow cane and vegetables. We'd grow sweet potato, beans, pumpkin, everything. We were made to share. On one farm, one uncle might have had too much of something on his farm, well he'd share it, he'd give it out, supply it to the mission. That's the way we were.

Today as I look around and see our young people, some of them are very greedy in many ways. Some of them don't believe in sharing, some of them do believe in sharing. They do things that they shouldn't do, getting up to all kinds of mischief that we didn't. But I say, those days on the island were the good old days to me.

The waratah and the pool of tears. Drawing by Lewis Walker.

I remember playing football with a tennis ball. The girls played the boys. Dorothy, my cousin, was pretty fast so we'd always throw the ball to her and she'd catch it and away she'd go. Then the boys would run to catch her and when they'd go to make a grab at her she'd palm them off. When they got closer she'd punch them, you know, she'd upper-cut them. She used to do all this. Then we'd come and follow up. Oh, we'd have a good game and we'd beat them every time, beat the boys every time.

The next round then, we'd have a game of hockey. The boys would make their own hockey sticks out of mangrove trees, not mango trees, but mangrove that grew all along the river bank. We'd have a game of hockey and the girls would always beat the boys, always. They were always beating the boys. The girls would come off best. Some of the boys would have busted ankles and everything.

So after that we'd be finished playing and we'd be all warmed up, real hot. We'd go and have a swim. Take our clothes off, the whole lot. It was nothing for us to swim naked because we didn't think anything of it, not like young people today. We just thought—well we had no swimmers those days so we just swam with no clothes on. Swimming around, no fear of sharks, no fear of anything. We were more or less a group of Aboriginal children on that island, enjoying the sun, enjoying life as we went on. It was so lovely and so beautiful, the island, green and beautiful.

Every Saturday morning we would go walking around the island and sometimes we'd find these fish. Their lungs would be all caught with slime, you know, the slime used to choke them. In certain years this would happen. The gills on the fish were all choked with slime. We'd take these fish home and show them to our Mum and Dad and tell them, 'Look here.' They'd say, 'Where you caught em?' Well we used to say, 'We just picked em up on the side.' They were only freshly dead, you know.

At all times we would bring the food in to help our Mum and Dad because we knew how hard it was. We often wondered where our next meal would come from but Mum would always have something on the table. She would cook damper bread or scone bread, this kind of food, never the loaf bread. We were always having damper. We used to get rations every second Thursday and it was only just a certain amount of rations. Not enough to last you till the next fortnight but only a certain amount that we had to make spin out.

Dad used to work over at Harwood for a chap called Mr Ryan. There was also another fellow down at Harwood Island, he used to help Dad a lot. His name was Archie Nicholson. All these people at Harwood, they were very good to Dad, even the Maclean people too, the town people. Dad was well respected by the white people and by the Aboriginal people round about him. He was a man of honesty, a very honest man. He was good, not only to the Aboriginal people but to the white people too. He loved his sport. He was a good cricketer. He was a great footballer. He was a bit of everything, and he was a man that you could trust. The white men used to trust him working on the farm. Even his boss would say, 'Well you stay here now, Rocky. I'm going to town. I won't be long.' So he used to stay and work on the farm and he was a very trusted man.

My Mum, she was a lovely person. She was a very good, very nice mother to us, to the girls and to the boys. She was always there when we needed her. And that's the beauty part of it, your mother is your best friend. When you've got a mother, always care for her. Show her that love because she's something precious, she's a jewel. She's something precious to you, she's your mother. She brought you into this world to look after you, to care for you. Always care about your mother and your father.

Anyway, during the school days there on the island we would have a big cooking day. On this day different people would come from different parts. Some of the Aboriginal people lived in town and they would come over. We would make cakes, brownies, damper bread, scones, a bit of everything. There were prizes given out to the best cooks. Mum would always win on the brownies, my aunty used to win on the oven breads and my other aunty was the best cake-maker. Everybody was something in that community. Even at Christmas time when people would come to the island they would make straight to our place. Course Dad always welcomed them there for a feed. There was a feed there at any time for anyone, any visitors.

There was a good few people used to live on the island those days, but they kept going out a little at a time, you know, kept moving off.

This one particular day, Dad went over to see the man who worked for the Aboriginal Protection Board about a boat. He wanted to ask them for a boat, a motor boat. He had two boats but they were rowing boats and they had just about had it. So when Dad went and saw this man he was told that they couldn't give him a boat. Dad was very downhearted and with us all growing up, he started to think, 'It'd be best if I was to move off this island.'

Before we moved off the island we used to go down to a place called Murrayville for our school holidays. Murrayville had little islands all about it and we spent a lot of our time swimming around them. We had a wonderful time down there. There were my mother, my father, my brothers and sisters and their wives and husbands. We'd all go and stay down at Murrayville and have a holiday. We would go fishing and hunting. We'd hunt for cobras (long wood worms up to two metres in length), get the log, pull it up and chop it up. Get the cobras out then take them home, cook them up and eat them. And we used to fish. We'd get the cobra logs and throw them back in the river. They would draw the bream. This is the way we caught our fish back in those days. We used to go back home to Mum and Dad with two big buckets of cobras and that would last us for a couple of meals. We had full and plenty.

Mum always bought bulk flour to take down. Big bags of plain flour, tins of baking powder, plenty of salt, plenty of pepper. Those days we used to get the big cans of syrup and big cans of honey. We didn't bother so much about the honey because we would get the wild honey. We'd go hunting for honey and lemons.

Every time someone got a cold we'd get a lemon, one that's not too juicy. Then we'd open the hot ashes out and put the lemon on the ashes and cover it over. This would draw all the juice out. We'd leave it there for about ten minutes then take it out and put it to one side to cool. After it's cool you cut it in half and all the juice is inside, all the goodness is inside. Then we'd put a spoonful of honey in the lemon and suck it that way because you're getting the beauty. Everything is in there with that lemon and the honey, and you're getting the lot. Oh, we used to often do that. We didn't know what it was like to have any kind of sickness because we were so healthy.

After the two weeks' holiday at Murrayville were up we would go back home to Ulgundahi Island just a couple of days before school started. At night we would sit around a big camp fire and Mum would tell us about the dreamtime. This certain story I remember quite well.

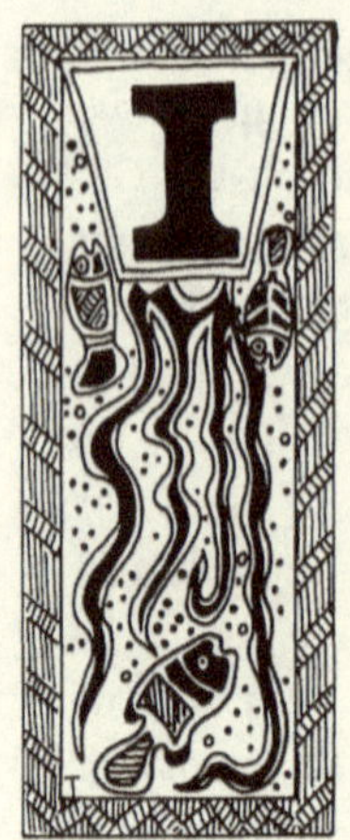

It's about a young Birrigan who lived at Iluka with his mother and his two sons. His wife had just died. Now, as his sons were growing up and getting older he started to think to himself, 'I'll have to go with my sons to another place.' He decided to go, so he made a bark canoe. He put his two sons in that canoe and away he went. His mother pleaded with him not to go, 'Don't go son, don't go. Stay here and look after me.' No, he had intentions of going to another place along the beach, so away he went.

As he was going out, further and further into the deep, his mother started to hit her yam stick on the water. She started to cry and sing out, 'Come back, come back! But the son didn't take any notice of his mother. He kept on going till he was out of sight.

She cursed the sea, she cursed it and the wind started to blow, the waves came higher. They were very frightened, the father and his two sons. Eventually it was too much for them and they drowned. Now, outside the place called Ballina there's three stones—the father, his two sons, and the nose part of the canoe sticking up. You can see them from the beach.

That's one of the stories she used to tell us. There were many, many more but that certain one I remember well. In the mornings before we went to school, we would carry water from an old well that was on the island. The water was heated in big boilers and we'd have our bath and get ready for school.

There were certain days when the men from the Aboriginal Protection Board would visit the island. The bigger boys and girls used to plant (hide). They'd say, 'He's comin to get me, he's comin to take me away.' Many's the time my father would have words with the Welfare who were out to take children from our family and many other families as well I remember my brother got taken away when he was a boy, to a boys' home. And when he came back, he came back a different man. He'd learnt to read and write and speak real nice but the Welfare just couldn't stop and think about our feelings, how my mother and father thought as human beings. It beats me how a person could just come and do what they liked to the families in those days. I still think about it today, how we were treated on the island by the Welfare.

Birrigan and his two sons on their way from Iluka. Drawing by Lewis Walker.

One flood time we had to stay on the island. We had no boat so Dad coo-eed out to Mr Bathgate, who lived nearby, to ring the police to come and pick us up. The police never came. My father, he just prayed. We had about four or five families in the one house. We shared that home with the rest of the people. We had nothing to eat. There was nothing in the house except a few onions. They couldn't come across to give us rations because it was too rough.

[inmage]

Well, it was just about dark when we saw this one hare on the island. My two brothers and the other boys, they ran that hare down. They caught it and skunted (skinned) it and cut it up. They opened up a big kerosene tin and put the hare in that. Meanwhile, us girls tucked our dresses up and waded over to the farm to dig around for potato and pumpkin. We went back and chopped that up with the onions to get enough to share with the others. We couldn't go and get any wood for a fire because all the wood was wet. We had to get some slabs that were in the kitchen and cut them up inside to make a fire so we could cook the supper. My mother and father fed all the families with that and everyone helped in.

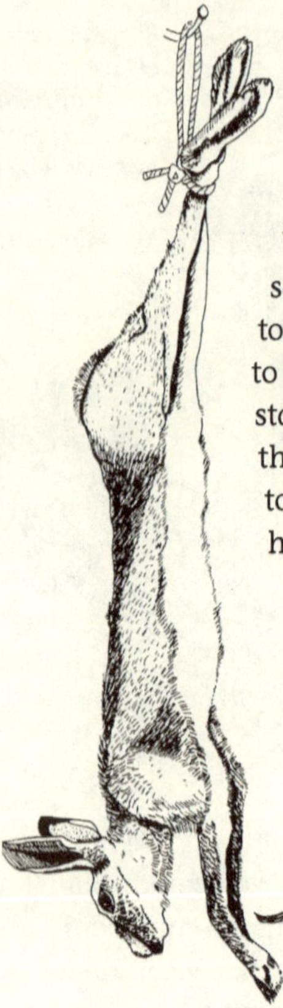

That same night we had a sing song. We said, 'Well let's just forget about the water, we'll have a sing song.' So we did and who came along, but my other cousin. He was in a boat and he rowed right to our front door. He said, 'Uncle Rocky, you not gonna sleep here tonight, are you?' 'Well boy, we got nowhere to go,' Dad said, 'we just gotta stay here.' So we stayed there that night and my father said to this boy, young Colin, he said, 'We gonna pray to God and believe God now, that he's gonna hold that water there. He won't let the water come in.' So, we had a sing song and my father prayed. He asked God to hold that water there till we went out of the house. He marked where the water was and the next morning when we got up that water hadn't risen and it hadn't gone down. It was the same!

As we were getting in the boat for Dad to row us down to this other little island where our Aunty Elsie and Uncle Georgie Randall lived, we had to look out for the snakes because they'd come and try to swim onto the little bit of island that wasn't under water. Rats and everything were trying to get onto that little place where we were. We had to kill them. So anyhow, just as Dad was the last fellow to leave the house, the water gushed in. It came in just like you were hosing it out. The water came straight into the house. Dad said, 'Well I thank you Lord for looking over us.' The police came then with the big boat to pick us up, but we had all gone!

Move to the mainland

When the flood was over we came back and that's when Dad decided to move off the island, because he had no help from the Aboriginal Protection Board, to help him with this motor boat that he wanted. The family was growing up and he decided to move. He packed up one of the rowing boats and rowed Mum and the smaller children down to a place called Whiting Beach near Yamba.

It was there that we stayed for about twelve months. Later on we moved into town. While we were at Whiting Beach my grandmother worked for Craigmore Guest House. It got too much for her so she gave the job to my Mum. Mum worked for Craigmore for a long, long time. She was the laundress. It was her job to boil all the sheets, starch and iron all the clothes. Everything had to be done perfect. I would go and help her on the weekends, do a little bit of whatever she wanted me to do. We had to put the linen through an old wooden mangler. Everything had to be dampened down then ironed a special way and the serviettes and uniforms were all starched to make them

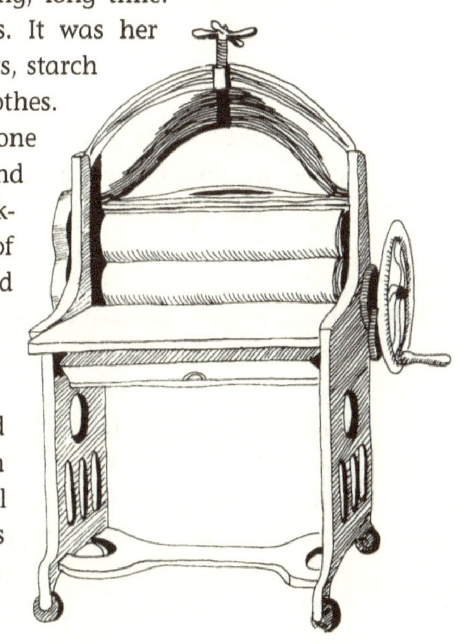

look nice. Mum worked very hard in the laundry. You see it was a great big house, Craigmore Guest House. It had one hundred and fifty rooms. If there was any food left over after lunch time, Mum was allowed to bring it home.

During her time there we moved into Yamba itself and I would go and work before school for people by the name of Teece—Henry and Mary Teece from Yamba. They had a beautiful family, they were just like my own. I was a part of them and they were a part of me. I'd start at seven o'clock in the morning, take my school clothes up there and have a shower. I'd send the boys to school first. There was Rexie, Gerald and Peter. These boys, I got very fond of them you know. Although I was a working girl there, I sort of felt that I was a part of that family.

Now today, there's only Mary Teece the mother, there's Doreen (now Doreen Castle) and the baby brother Peter still alive. I haven't seen Peter since I've grown up and married. I haven't seen him at all but I'd like to see him. I saw Doreen a couple of times, went to her house and had a yarn. I saw her husband, Kevin Castle, and it was so nice. We'd sit down and talk about the old days and laugh and cry. Tears would come into my eyes with joy to know that I had someone to talk to, that I could relate to as a friend, as a person who understood me, who understood my ways, who understood the Aboriginal people. She was my friend and her family was my family too. They were my good friends and still today, Doreen is a very lovely person. She's still got that laugh that she had years and years ago. She used to call me Nella. She is a great, great, lovely person and her husband Kevin, he too is a very nice man. Doreen often talked about Dad, she didn't see so much of Mum. She said that Dad was a well respected man in that community.

I loved working for the Teeces. After I got the boys off to school I'd make the beds, dust and polish the furniture, help Doreen do little things in the house. It was nothing for me to do those kinds of things because I just loved doing them.

When I finished the housework I would hear the school bell ringing. The first bell used to ring, well I was ready and I'd run down the hill. It was all sandy from the Teece's place to way down the bottom. I would run down to the Teece's shop. One side was a butcher shop and the other side was a fruit and vegetable shop. Mrs Teece gave me fruit to take to school. I worked for a long time but I had to do it to help my mother and father. You see, it was hard for Dad, cause all he could do to bring the money in, was to catch worms, My Dad, he was everything to me.

Dad was always busy. He would go fishing or sometimes he would go and catch sea worms. Holiday time he would get these orders. Certain ones used to say, 'Oh Rocky, would you get me some sea worms, about four or five pounds of worms?' Dad would go and make himself busy. We had a horse named Bobby, Dad used to ride it right out to Shelley Beach to get the orders. He'd come back with two or three cans full of worms and do them up in paper packets, then sell them for so much a packet. That's how we made money, with the worms that he caught along the beach. We'd all go down and watch him. He'd show us how to catch them, then we'd have a go. Now they're all great worm-catchers, my nieces and nephews too.

My brother Raymond was very special to me. He was a runner and we trained together. I was his pace-marker and I was always there to run up and down the sand with him.

Rowing family to Whiting Beach

He'd give me a start and I would beat him to the sandhills but I couldn't beat him up the hills. He beat me every time. We trained him to go to Coffs Harbour and other places all over the North Coast, foot racing. One day there was a great big sports carnival down here at Maclean Showground. Four or five of my brothers were in this race and they had to run around the showground. There was a very fast runner from Grafton—one of the Ferguson boys who came down and competed. Raymond won the race. He was pretty fast. He was a good, happy-go-lucky boy, happy-go-lucky man he was. When he died he left a family of eight.

Looking back on those years, they were very, very happy days for me and my brothers. I was a real tomboy and I often ran with them. Whatever the boys did, I did too. I played cricket and football with them. I'd run with them or jog with them. I think about those times because, well you never see young mothers today or even brothers and sisters running around and enjoying life the way we used to. You never see that today but those days were happy days for me.

We had huts all over the place. We moved here, we moved there. All along Angourie Road we lived. Every place that we stayed in at Yamba, we had to move from. The Urban Area (now the local council) wanted to clean the place up. They were always putting in new developments. And we lived all along there, from where the golf course is right to where the new homes are now at Pippi Beach. We were quite happy there. Then, again we were told that we had to move to another place. It was hard when we had to move all the time.

There was a big swamp at the back of what is now the golf

club and every Christmas time masses of flowers grew there. We used to go and get bunches and bunches of Christmas Bells and Boronias. Then we'd take them to Craigmore and to different houses in the town and sell them. They would give us ten shillings for the biggest bunch of flowers. Every Christmas time we'd have these orders. When my Dad wandered around Yamba there, if he didn't catch many worms he'd come home with flowers to sell so Mum could buy bread or meat. You know, I look at some of the young ones today and I see how they don't appreciate their mother and father but we thought there was nobody like our mother and father. They always saw that we had something to eat.

When I went to school we used to buy a loaf of bread in the afternoon and go down to the rocks and have a feed of oysters with the dry bread, just the oysters from the rocks. We didn't go without a feed. We knew there was food there. There were pippies, there were oysters, always something for us to eat. One day Dad went down to the quarry and he caught this great big jewfish and then he caught another jewfish. They were nearly bigger than himself. When he carried them home the tail parts were still dragging. He had them in a big sugar bag, that's the only way that he could carry them. After that the boys would always go with him and when he caught the big fish they would help him carry them home.

As life went on and I worked around the Yamba area, I was about fourteen when I decided that I couldn't learn any more. I thought that education was nothing I thought, 'I'm a big girl now, I can't learn anymore.' So I decided to leave school to work full time, which I did. When I did work I liked it because I knew I was doing something and I thought that education was nothing. I worked hard. My knees would get sore from scrubbing and polishing the floors. I did the dusting, cleaned the windows, I washed and ironed and polished shoes. That was all a part of my job. When I went home after work I had to wash and iron my own clothes. I didn't do my ironing with an electric iron but with an old stove iron. The old-fashioned ones that you had to clean up first so no black soot or anything could get on your clothes. I didn't mind the work because they were my friends—the Teece family.

We stayed in Yamba till I was seventeen years of age and then we moved. But I must tell you this first. When I was at Whiting Beach before we moved into town, we used to play marbles. We'd play marbles with the pearls that we got out of oysters. Course we never did think that they were something special. To me they were just marbles. Never ever thought that they were real pearls from the oysters. We thought nothing, we just played marbles with the pearls. So you know, those days we didn't realise they were precious and I suppose something that somebody else would treasure.

Dad would call us up from the beach where we played. He'd sing out, 'Come on, it's getting late now Come back up here.' We'd come back up and Mum would have our supper cooked. It was a big ashes damper with butter and syrup, syrup was our main meal. We always had syrup with ashes bread and fish. We didn't ask for anything else. We weren't particular and never said, 'Oh, I don't want that I want this.' We had no choice. We had to eat what was put in front of us. We were told to eat it I see kids today, they're not thankful or they're not satisfied with what they eat. They're very particular, 'I don't want this, I don't want that.' We had to eat what was put in front of us.

The Casino Aboriginal people often came over. Every Christmas time they used to come down to Yamba and have the whole six weeks there. We'd play games at night time. There were big sandhills and, oh, how we enjoyed ourselves. There were about sixty or seventy, I suppose, used to come two big truck loads full of our Aboriginal people from over at Casino. And they used to enjoy their holidays. We'd go to the beach gathering pippies and oysters. We thought that it was lovely. When our friends came from Casino we were overjoyed to see them. And it was there that I came to know the friends I have now.

I had a mate, Patti, she was my good friend. Now today, she's gone. She died at a young age. I always think about the times when we used to go playing or hunting. They were good times, us girls had fun. Never hung around our mother and father, we'd just go and enjoy ourselves because it was holiday time and we wanted to meet people. We wanted to enjoy ourselves, not getting up to mischief, not doing things that we shouldn't do but enjoying the holiday, the sun, the people. That's what life is all about. It was so lovely. I felt so free. You feel like everything around you is so beautiful. Oh it was lovely to go and enjoy ourselves, to laugh with our friends. It was just wonderful.

Sometimes we'd have a game of poker. Penny-a-go to buy poker. We used to have a good game. And this old lady, she used to beat us every time. To me it was more or less a fun game, you know. Everybody would bring their pennies and the old girl would beat us every time, the old girl from Casino. We didn't gamble for big money. It was just penny-a-go, buy a poker. After she won the money off us she used to turn around and give us each so much back. Then we'd go and buy an iceblock or something that we really wanted. She used to give all the money back to us. I was just wondering, would we have given her the money if we had won off her, you know!

Life to me, it wasn't that hard and I see my people now, our Aboriginal people, our young ones, they can't satisfy themselves. They're doing things we never ever did in our life. All we wanted to live for was to enjoy life, enjoy day-to-day living. It's something that I can say, it's good that I can tell you this about my people, those I grew up with. We were a happy lot of people. When I lived at Yamba with my brothers and sisters we were all happy. We were always joking and laughing, always full of life. We had fun. We never used to fight because we had that love for one another. We know that love is everything in the family, in the family home. When you've got that love, you've got everything. It's so wonderful!

Recollections by Doreen Castle

You know the old water tanks, well Della's people lived in those cut in half. I'd say poor old Sandy Cameron (Della's uncle) had the best. He had a tin shed. Oh, when it rained they used to leak and after it'd fine up, you'd see all the clothes go out, you know, all the drying to do. It was terrible. They didn't get the help they get now. Not that I begrudge them that, but they didn't get any help at all. They only got what they earned. The men used to try and do a little bit of cane work or they'd go out worming and the older women would go out to wash or do a little bit here and there. Well, I suppose things were hard for everybody but it seemed terribly hard for them I don't know why.

Dad owned a butcher shop and a fruit and vegetable shop. The girls all worked and Mum found it hard with the boys at home. That's how Della came to work for us. Dad got her to come up and she used to get the boys out of bed. I was talking to my brother, Peter, on the phone and he roared with laughter. You see we always called our brother Gerald, 'Charlie'; and he said, 'Poor old Charlie'. Many a time Della would say, 'I'll throw a bucket of water over you if you don't get up.' He was terrible to get out of bed. Anyhow she'd get them up and ready for school. Then she'd make the beds and tidy up. Then she'd come and get her money and go to school.

My brothers all went to the convent and Della went to the public school down on the flat. Well, it's still in the same spot. But that's how Della came to work for us. She was only about fourteen then. We got very attached to her. She'd come about half past seven and leave about ten to nine as she was still going to school. I don't know how long she worked for us. It was a long time and we got to really love her.

I'm older than Della I was working when she worked for us. She worked on weekends and every day in the mornings. I was trying to remember how much she got. I know it wasn't a lot of money. She'd come and get her money and Dad would tell her to come back after school and he'd always have a bit of scrap meat. Mum would have scrap fruit and things for her, to help them out because they were really hungry. I don't know, it's hard to explain what it was like for them in those days.

The only pair of shoes that I think Della ever had was a pair I gave her. I never saw shoes on her feet. They even went to school without shoes. It was so cold and I remember saying, Would these fit you?' I can still see it. She thought they were marvellous. She came out next morning with them on. Anything you gave her, she was grateful for.

They had a lot of fun, you know, and she learned to love them, my brothers, as much as they loved her. She classed us as family, I think, in the finish. She got to know us so well. We made her a part of us. The kids played together. It was different then. The kids all played on the flat there and the Aboriginal children would come in and play with us. We never thought it was anything different. There were a few whites that wouldn't let their children mix but my parents never worried. As long as they could see us and we were playing, it was okay. That's all they worried about.

I remember my sister, Narelle and I used to sleep in a double bed and we had to make it ourselves when we started to work. That was the law, that we made our own bed. One day Narelle and I had an argument. We were thick (close) but we'd had an argument over something and Narelle said, Well, it's your tum to make the bed.' I said, 'I'm not making your half.' I can't even remember what we argued over I can remember Della standing at the door, looking at me and laughing at me, laughing like anything. It took me longer to just make my half of the bed than to make the whole thing. I can still see this skinny little thing standing there roaring. She thought it was a great joke that I would make my half of the bed and leave Narelle's half. She used to think things like this were marvellous and she was such a good little worker. She worked hard, she really did. Then I think she went to Craigmore and did the washing at times. I think she was trying to help out at home because it was a

big family. There were a lot of younger ones too, about fourteen or fifteen of them.

The whole family were good athletes, too, including Della at school. I know she was good at running. She was really good. I can remember Peter and Gerald and 'Tiger' Rex as we called him, trying to race her. 'We can beat you,' they'd say. Well she'd leave them for dead. I can remember playing rounders with her. We were very close. I don't know, I suppose we didn't grow up as fast as the kids do today. Like if I was fourteen I'd play with the kids who were only six or seven year olds. Oh yes, we used to play. I remember the hill, we call it now, it went straight up past our place. Well at that time it was just a sandhill and down the bottom it was all grassy flats. Everyone gathered there after school for a game of rounders. This was when Della was younger, before she came to work for Dad. Of course when I got too big to play, I used to watch them from work.

Oh, but they had it tough I don't think anyone realised how tough. There were more than the Lauries, there were lots of families that were out on the racecourse, as we call it. In the wet weather the racecourse would swamp so they camped on this hill, a big ridge. I'd call it 'camped' because that's what it was. They were always moving on. Then they tried to get them to stay on the island. But see the floods came and they nearly lost lives and everything then. It was nearly impossible to get children to school and everything, really. It was so isolated and cars weren't like they are today. Today, nearly everybody has a car, but if you had one in those days you were considered a rich person.

Well, to my way of speaking, I think Della was a very honest, real to life person. She was married young but she was a good mother. She loved life and loved her family. I really do think *that. My brother Peter, said on the phone, 'Gee, she was an unreal person,' and that's my summing up of her. She was an unreal person, not 'was' I should say, but 'is' an unreal person. When she was young, she had long black curly hair and such lovely white teeth and she always had this big smile. She'd sing out when she got to work, 'I'm here,' and she would always hang her head. See, she's not shy now, but in those days she was. Well, she'd hang her head but she would always have this big grin on her face. I* think *the reason why she took to us was that Mum and Dad treated her just like us, as if she was one of us.*

Move to Tabulam

Later on we moved to Tabulam, a little place way up in the bush. It's a lovely place, nice little town between Casino and Tenterfield. It was there that my father got a job out at the Plains Station. A man from Harwood Island got Dad a job on the farm milking cows and looking after the cattle. We all moved up to help Dad with the work. We thought it was lovely out there because it was so quiet. We would get up early on the cold and frosty mornings to fetch the cows in to put them in the yard while Dad and the other boys made a fire in the dairy. We all did our little bit to help Mum and Dad.

My little sister went to school in Tabulam. It was hard to get into town from where we lived, into the shopping place but it was so beautiful. It was all bush country and a very lovely place. We used to go fishing down on the river bank, all fresh water. It's the Upper Clarence, inland. Anyhow we would go fishing and catch catfish, eels, turtles, perch and cod. It was lovely just to sit down and relax on the river bank. We'd take the tea and sugar down and brew up a cup of tea because it was all fresh water. I really enjoyed myself at the Plains Station.

After we finished with the cows we would feed the pigs. There was one little pig that the boss gave to my sister, Lillian. He said to her, 'You can have this pig.' She called him Mango. I had a pig and my other sister had a pig too, but Lillian's little pig, we would get it out of the sty and bathe it and clean it then let it way out on the farm. Oh, he looked so beautiful and clean. We just used to let him lay down in the sun and sun himself. Then when we'd go to look for this pig again he'd be all muddy. He'd be covered in it and you could just

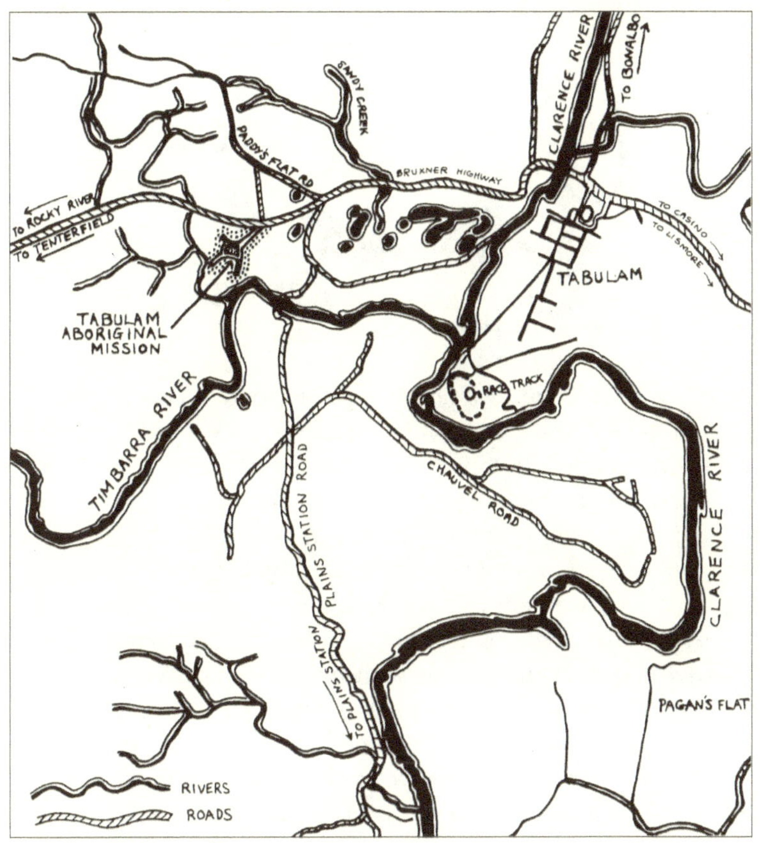

Map of Tabulam and the surrounding area. Drawn by Tryphena McShane.

see these two eyes peeking at you through the mud. My sister would try to catch him but he'd lay right down in the mud up to his neck and just look at us. Dear we had some fun trying to get him away from the mud.

One time the brothers went hunting and they caught this baby kangaroo. We had it there for a good while. So there were the pigs and this joey that we had, not counting the dogs and the cats. We had full and plenty there to feed them on. There was milk and meat and a bit of vegies in the garden for the pigs.

My sisters and I would often go walkabout. One day Dad said to us, 'Don't you go into Tabulam.' We wanted to sneak in and watch the football on Sunday afternoon. He said, 'Don't you go sneaking off to the football because if I've got to go after you, look out.' So we walked about two miles up the road and we kept in our memory that Dad was going to chase us if we went into the football. We thought, 'He'll get us. We'll get a hiding for sure.' We were too frightened to do anything we shouldn't, see, so away we came back again. We were on our way back and Mavis said, 'It'd be funny if this truck that's coming pulled up and asked us if we wanted a lift into Tabulam. What would you say?' I said, 'Oh no, we can't.' And the funny thing is, just what my sister said, that's what happened. This chap stopped and asked us if we'd like a lift. 'Oh, no thank you, we's just walking about.' Away we went back down to Mum and Dad again. See, we took notice of what our father told us.

We grabbed some lines and went down to the river bank. I caught this great big huge eel. It gave me a fright. I'd never ever seen a fresh water eel before. He's different to a salt water eel, you know. He's sort of a brownish black but the salt water eel is green, like a liver colour. When I started pulling him in he was thrashing around. We pulled him onto the bank and sang out to my brothers and their mates who were about two hundred yards down the river, 'Come here and look what we caught.' I said, 'Is this an eel or what?' You know, cause this was the first time I'd seen one. 'Yeah, that's an eel,' they said. 'Well are we going to take him home and cook him?' 'Oh no, he's too big, don't take that,' this other cousin said to me. Like, you hear so many things about different places, different Aboriginal traditions. Don't do this or don't touch that. We had this in our head, see. We thought the eel might be special to these parts. Oh, he was a great big lovely eel. We took it home and showed Mum. She sliced it up and cooked it and fed it to the pigs. We didn't know then that you could fry them up all nice. We just boiled it and fed it to the pigs.

About three o'clock we'd get the cows in again for milking, then help Dad to separate the cream. One morning I was taking the cans on a cart slide out to the road to catch the cream truck. As I was going out this horse started to trot. We hit a bump and one cream can tipped over. I got frightened so I yelled out to Dad. Dad and the boys came and I got roused on for doing a thing like that. That horse was so stubborn he would sometimes go backwards. I said to the brothers, 'You'd better take the cream out from now on, I won't do it. I've already lost one full can.' Dad let the boys take it from then on. My job with the other sisters, was to get up very early in the morning and fetch the cows in for milking, about fifty or sixty head. We'd muster them up then let them out till three o'clock when we did the milking again. Between nine and three we would do whatever Mum wanted of us around the house, clean up or help prepare the meals.

One time we caught a cold. Every one of us had a cold. Alan, my brother, got a big lot of lemons from the tree down the road and he made us all a hot lemon drink in the billy can. He put a little bit of sugar, a pinch of salt and two teaspoons of metho in each drink, stirred it up and gave it to us with an aspirin. We were so sick with this cold. You know how sometimes you just can't get out of bed in the morning. We all stayed in bed and had this drink with an aspirin then we started sweating. It poured off us so that we were all soaking wet. The next morning we were as good as gold, every one of us. We had that drink all the time then. It wasn't just the metho, we used to put the wild honey in instead of sugar and it would clear all the phlegm off the chest, clear it all off.

Then the boss sold the farm and we moved to a property on the Rocky River, Claude Winterton's place. We lived there in a three bedroom home with my mother's cousin, Clarrie Hookey. We stayed there for, oh, it was over two years, I suppose. That's where I first met my husband. He used to come and do some mustering. We'd have a bit of a talk. So anyhow we got real serious with one another, I fell in love with him and he fell in love with me. We started going out then. He lived over at a place called Merrica that I had to pass by on my way to town.

By this time I had a job in town at the Braid's place. He owned the Tabulam Butcher Shop and I did the work for his wife. I did the washing and ironing and house cleaning. They were very nice to me, the Braid family. I worked there for about six months and on the way I would go and see my boyfriend, the man I fell in love with. I became pregnant for the first time so we moved down to Turtle Point. That's the old mission at the back of Tabulam township. This was right on the Clarence River again and where my eldest son was born. It was a nice little place but a bit steep when we'd take a short-cut home from town. There was plenty of corn growing there in those days. We would go to a place called The Little Top overlooking the corn paddocks across to the place called Merrica where the other Aboriginal people lived, my husband's mother and grandmother and Uncle Sam Walker.

It was on 14 June that I had my first baby. I'd had a good feed of corn and a good feed of lemons. I thought this had upset my stomach. I didn't know anything about babies or anything about the pains. I wasn't told when to expect the pains or anything. I just thought I had diarrhoea. I was in and out, in and out. We were staying with Mrs Donnelly at the time. She was my husband's cousin. She said to me, 'Tida, you not gibin?' 'No, no,' I said. 'Oh, I'm sure you must be.' She'd said to me, 'You not gibin?' That means, 'You're not sick?' I thought it was just diarrhoea but it wasn't. It was the labour pains coming. I didn't know anything. I kept going out, back and forward, back and forward and it was one of those old-fashioned toilets. About seven o'clock that evening Lenny was born. He was a beautiful baby, born very clean. My cousin Lottie, she looked after me. She did all the work that the doctors do in hospital. I still had to go in the ambulance to Casino and I rested there for about a week. When I came home I found that I had a responsibility. I had to look after and care for that baby.

We used to stay all along the river bank. Make a little humpy then put a bag over on top of that again. Then we'd make a little bed on the grass for myself, my husband and the baby. We kept on living like that for oh, months and months and months, here and there just travelling with the baby. He was starting to grow, getting nice and big, so I would go with my husband to help him pull the corn. We'd leave the little fella with my husband's mother and father. All over the place we'd go pulling corn, then when we came home at night I'd be real tired. I'd do all his washing in the night time then go again to work the next morning. It kept going on like this and the years started passing by—1950, 1951—that was the year he was born. Then he started to grow—1952, 1953 and I became pregnant again. I had my second child, a little girl called Narelle.

We were in the mission at this stage, the new settlement. The managers came and moved the people off the old mission and into the new one that's still there now. There were eighteen new homes and all the people that moved onto the new reserve had their pride. They were proud of their new homes, their vegetable gardens and flower gardens. There was one garden there my sister-in-law Adelaide had, and one onion weighed two pounds. They had it on show at Murray's Café. We had all different kinds of vegetables growing there. Everybody was independent. They had their new homes and they had pride in them. People had lemon trees and some had orange trees, and talk about beautiful flower gardens! They used to give prizes for the best flower garden.

There were also horses on the reserve and my husband was a great horseman. We had cattle too. My husband helped with the mustering and weaning. My eldest son, he was the greatest. He only had to break in a horse for say a week, then he'd be on that horse. That's the kind of boy he was. He was a lovely rider, wasn't frightened.

About this time my little baby girl got sick. She had pneumonia, bronchitis, whooping cough. You see, when we were living in the old ways there was hardly anything like that, but the minute we came into a good home we started getting sick. We were under a white manager then and when people got the sickness they would go over every morning to get treated. When Narelle got real sick and we had to rush her to the Casino Memorial Hospital. The doctor said to me, 'Don't worry, she's going to be alright.' I looked around and saw all the things that they had in there and saw that the nurses and sisters were really nice people. So I left her in that hospital and away I came, back to Tabulam. She was in there for three weeks. When she came home from hospital she was a healthy little girl. I was so proud of her. Her nickname is China.

While my husband was at work we used to get this old draught horse we had on the mission, called Toby, and put him to a cart to get the firewood. Certain mornings we'd go up to the old saleyards for the wood and then when we had the cart all loaded up, instead of going forwards the horse used to go backwards. Well, we didn't know what to do. We just didn't know how to make this horse go forwards. Different days, different women would go to get the wood and this particular day there was a young girl with us by the name of Alma Wilson, only a teenager she was. She said to us, 'I'll drive the cart and you oldies can walk' 'Yeah,' I said, 'We'll walk.' So we started to walk behind the cart. It was then the horse started to bolt. I don't know whatever happened. After it bolted through the trees for about twenty yards it just stopped, just stood there with all this wood in the cart. And do you think that we could move that horse? We couldn't!

There was a road nearby and these two men came along. Jeffrey Phillips and the chap he worked for, Jack Daly. They saw us there trying to get this Toby to come. It was about five o'clock in the evening by this time. Some of us were pulling and some were pushing. Jack Daly jumped out of his truck and he started to swear. He said, 'I'll get him to go. I'll make a fire underneath him.' He was really going to make this fire, so he heaped up a little bit of bramble and some leaves and got it all fixed up. This girl, named Alma Wilson, she was standing there and she was watching, see. She said, 'Oh please Mr Daly, don't do that. That's government property.' He said, 'I'll fix this horse, I'm gonna make him trot.'

We had to take the harness and everything off that horse cause he just wouldn't budge. We couldn't make a fire underneath him cause he was government property, so we went home. We had to leave the cart there with all the wood on and go home to get someone else. The handyman came and harnessed the horse up again to the cart and brought all the wood back down to where I lived. He got the horse to go but we couldn't. We had a lovely big fire that night and I just laughed and laughed and laughed to think of the way Alma said, 'That's government property.' Jack Daly said, 'I don't care if it's government property or not, I'll burn it.' Well you should have seen the look on her face!

Motherhood

In the mornings after we gathered the wood we went out and did the garden, raked up around the house and cleaned the yard up. Then we went down the back and heaped all the rubbish up and we made a big fire. Then I got the kiddies off to school. It wasn't far. I could see them walking over to the school house. It was on the Aboriginal reserve at Tabulam. You could see the kiddies having their sports at lunch time. We used to talk to the teacher about how they were coming along with their schooling. The teacher was very proud of the kiddies because they won two or three contests with their singing. He took them to Lismore to the big festivals. He was a very nice teacher, Austin Soorley. His sister was the matron and her husband was the manager in those days.

About that time my husband got a job at the asbestos mines at Baryulgil. He worked on the jack hammers at the mines for six years. He would come home Friday and go back Sunday evening. He worked very hard at the mines. It wasn't a lot of money, just enough to keep the family going. When he'd come home of a Friday afternoon I would go and get the groceries, keeping just enough money for petrol to get him back to work for the Monday. This went on and on.

We couldn't save any money because we had a family and it was a big family. It took all our money to feed them. They were given ration clothes those days but I couldn't get any for my kiddies because their father worked. We struggled. It was a tough time and it was hard for the children to understand. If we were out of food we couldn't just go to the shop and book it up. It was a funny town in those days. Everybody knew one another's business. Everybody watched one another but life still went on.

My husband worked hard for his family. I loved him very much. One day he helped me when I was sick. I got sick with blood pressure and I couldn't get up to do anything. If I tried to stand I would get dizzy, my head would throb I could see the stars in front of me. He stayed home this particular day and he said to me, 'Well Mum, you just stay there on the bed, I'll do things around the house for you.' He made some scones and he cooked the stew. Then he called out to the kiddies and fed them I was very proud of him for doing that.

My second son, John, was a little toddler then and I was pregnant with my next child. There was a year between all my children I sort of grew up with them. They understood my ways and I understood them because I was such a young mother myself. Fourteen kiddies I had, four girls and ten boys. Eighteen I was when I had my first son. Then almost every year there was another one coming along I managed with my babies though it wasn't easy.

Often times the pump would break down and we had no water. We would go down to the river to wash, taking opened kerosene buckets for boilers. We'd light a big fire and boil our clothes down there at the river. Then we would throw them over the trees or over the fences. Anywhere that our clothes would dry, we'd have them hanging. It would take two or three trips back up the hill to our houses with all these lovely, clean, dry clothes. We really had no worries then. Always found a way to do things. We used to do it because we wanted our clothes and our houses nice and clean.

The manager's wife would come around and visit the houses every Thursday or sometimes on Tuesday mornings she would do the rounds. We could see her coming, prowling around and we'd yell out, 'She's a comin.' Well, you'd see the people running with mops and brooms to clean the place up. She'd start at house number one and make her way up the street. My house was number five.

Anyhow, one day when she came I was sweeping out the kitchen, scrubbing it with the broom. I knew she was coming but I didn't think she would get to my place so quick. I'd scrubbed the other rooms out and was just finishing sweeping the water out the kitchen door—cause they were all bare floors—when the water met her at the door. 'Oh!' she said, 'Goodness gracious me Della, what are you doing?' I said, 'Well I'm cleaning the place up and you're in my way. Would you please step aside?' So she stepped aside and she said, 'Oh, goodness gracious me! This is just like the first house, the place is all wet.' 'Well,' I said, 'It's cleaning up day. We've decided to clean up early in the morning. I'm not trying to be rude or nothing but you know, you're in the way.' She had a bit of a yarn to me then and away she went up the street.

We knew that a house had to be cleaned every day, not just certain days and we kept it that way. We always took pride in our homes. They were new homes you know, and we looked after them to the best of our ability. She was one of those straight out old ladies. She would speak her mind, no back door with her. She was one of those kind of women that you could joke with and laugh with. When she and her husband left the mission there was another lot came. Every two or three years another lot would come.

Back then, I used to go over to the manager's wife every second Thursday to scrub the floors, scrub the bricks outside, mop the treatment room, anything I could put my hands to I'd do all this for a ration of flour, baking powder, tea, butter, meat and milk. That was our allowance for the next fortnight

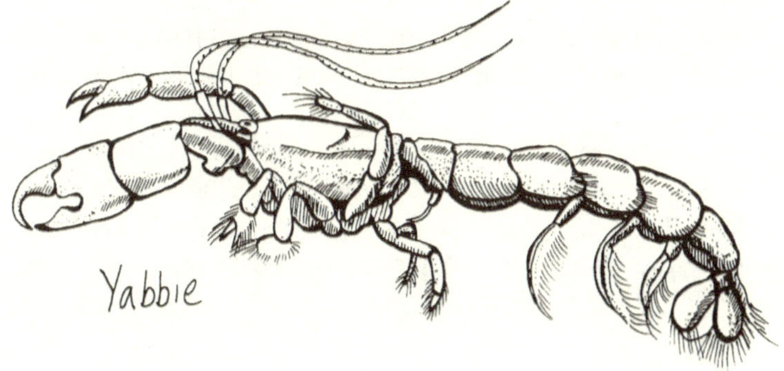

but it wasn't enough. What used to help us was that the boys would go hunting for food. It was the wild food that helped the family get by. As the years went on everything got hard. It got harder and harder.

You couldn't walk into a pub in those days back in the 1950s. You couldn't do what you liked, not like the young people today. The boss would give all the working men a small bottle of wine. Many's the time I saw what they did, how they would give the men the alcohol. Then later on the exemption cards came out. If you had one of them you could go into the pub then. You had to be recognised with your photo in the corner.

During these hard times I started going to bible study. It helped me to know there was a Saviour looking over us all. It worried me though that I was not married in the eyes of the Lord. I'd already had four babies and it was important to me that they have their father's name. We decided to get married. My Mum and Dad came up for the wedding. We had a great big *'do'*. Everybody was invited. Oh, there was about two or three hundred at the wedding!

We used the big hall that was at the comer of the mission. It was beautiful. It had a big stage and all the tables were set out with food. All my people came up from Maclean, my cousins, my aunties and uncles. They were all there. We had a beautiful wedding but there was no dancing or disco. It was a big church gathering we had. It was just wonderful to see everybody singing, everybody happy I was overjoyed. I was expecting my fifth child, Ricky, by this time. I had a beautiful wedding dress made for me. Oh and all the lovely presents we got.

After the service we drove around the square at the mission in our old car. We thought it was one of the best cars in those days. It was an old Ford and we just thought it was beautiful to sit and wave at the people, blowing the horn as we went around. You see, when Aboriginal people have a wedding everybody's invited. Don't care who they are or what they are, they come along and they enjoy themselves. Getting together with the other people and talking and laughing. That's the way that life is. It's the way we are.

And as life goes on today, you can see that there is a great change in the people, a great change in the way of living, far different to the days when I was a young mother. When I look back on those days I say to myself, 'My, how things have changed. My sons, my daughters, how they've changed.'

The second daughter of mine, she died when she was three years of age—an accident with the pram. She was nursing young Ricky. He was a huge baby, big and fat and solid. My little nephew was taking them for a walk and she was nursing Ricky. She had her arms around him, cuddling him. I was busy in the laundry and not thinking or knowing what was going on because I was busy washing. I had the big coppers lit boiling the clothes. I couldn't afford a washing machine with all the family that I had. I heard the little girl crying, about three or four o'clock in the afternoon it was. I rushed out and saw the pram upside down. Ricky was lying on top of her. She'd hurt her back when he had fallen on her with his weight I didn't realise she was so hurt. Just didn't think because she cried only for a little while and then she went to sleep. I said, 'You alright?' And she was nodding her head, see.

That night I gave her tea and she ate then went back to sleep and she never woke up till the next morning. About seven o'clock she got up but she couldn't sit down. I raced straight over to the manager's place, then to Matron Levin and told her. She said to me, 'Well Della, you take that little one straight over to the Lismore Hospital.' So I took her—miles away it was. The doctor said to me, 'I don't want you to go too far, you can't go home. Your little one is a very sick girl.' I rang my husband who was at work at the asbestos mines at Baryulgil—miles away. Soon as he knocked off work he came straight down. We spent the night in Lismore, that was on the Wednesday. Thursday night at seven o'clock she passed away.

It was sad for me because it was my baby girl that I really loved. She was always sickly though. She wasn't a healthy little thing, always in and out of hospital. The thing is, she was just starting to pick up with her health when that happened, but I suppose there's a reason God gives, He takes, you know, and I can't question that. I can't say anything about that because like, you know what I mean, I suppose she just wasn't meant to grow. She was meant to go back. I suppose God gives, He takes, and we should never question God cause He knows best.

As life went on I couldn't open myself to anything, I just couldn't. My mind used to wander and I'd grab a bag and go across the gully when my husband was at work. I'd grab a bag and go across by myself just to get away, just to get it out of my mind. It was there all the time, in my mind and I used to try and work it out. I found that was the only way I could do it, but it's still there, no matter what you try to do. It will always be there. When I said to that little boy David, 'Now, you had no right to put her in the pram like that,' he said, 'I didn't know Ma Walker, I'm sorry.' Poor mite, he didn't know the damage that would happen. I don't know, I suppose it was meant to be.

Then the other little one came along. I had a boy next to her passing, and today she would have been a big girl. I had another son. I kept on trying to have a girl but I kept on having sons. I had these ten boys and only four girls. Now I'm very pleased and I thank God for giving me the strength to go on seeing my children grow up, to be young men and women. That they are strong and have always been taught what is right, never learnt to be greedy. Always learnt to give and to share. That's the way they were brought up to be because that's the way I was brought up to be.

My husband worked at the mines till about 1958, then he hurt his back. He had three weeks off and when he went back he got no compensation or nothing from the asbestos mines. He got nothing for hurting his back. For years and years this went on, with him working very hard and then when he hurt himself, nothing. He loved his work, he loved having a job but the time had come when he couldn't work anymore. He just couldn't. The old back couldn't take it any longer. He stayed home then and was on sickness benefit for about two years.

The work he used to do down there on the jack hammer, it was hard. His clothes would be as stiff as anything when he came home. They were snow white with the dust. He used to tie his hanky at the four comers and make a hat out of it. Around his eyebrows and eyelashes was all just snow white. His shoes and socks would be full of it, spiky asbestos, just like little needles. I'd soak his clothes overnight and then I'd get a scrubbing brush to them. I couldn't touch them with my hands because all the prickles would stick in me.

When he hurt his back at the mines was the time I really felt it. I felt so helpless. I couldn't do anything for him He was going to a certain doctor at Bonalbo who was the first person to see him when he hurt his back. The doctor wouldn't believe that my husband was sick so he went to a doctor in Casino after that. Later he went back to the mines to work but he couldn't. The back used to come against him. It used to hurt him too much so he knocked it in the head. In 1969 he put in for the invalid pension and we got pensioned. In 1970 we moved from the reserve at Tabulam to Bonalbo.

Now I look around up here at Tabulam and I see the ones I met when I first moved here and I see their families growing, and their families again. It's wonderful how they looked after me and how I looked after myself. I took great care of myself. I respected myself as a woman and I'm so proud that I am what I am. I want everybody to know what it's like to struggle in life, how I battled and had to go on battling for my rights. And I've got the right to say what I need to say to people. Being a mother of fourteen, every little penny counts. How the money goes! What I've got to say comes direct from the heart. This story, it's true. It's not made up what I'm telling you in this book. I want everyone to know how I struggled to raise my family. Working here and there just to fetch food home for my children. Barely had any education, yet I can hold my head up high and say, 'I am what I am, an Aboriginal woman.'

Recollections by Adelaide

When I first met Della she was only a teenager. She used to live across the Rocky River and I used to live on the Clarence River. We'd meet halfway and play on the road and in the corn paddock. Then we'd go down the river and play there till it was time to come home. Della had to walk across the river back over to the Rocky to where she was staying and we'd all go back to our place till again the next day, it'd be like that. We didn't even know what her name was. We used to call her 'mate'. We didn't know her name was Della till a couple of days after. She got used to us then. That's where she met my brother, William.

We used to go to the old mission then, the place they call Turtle Point. That was before this new mission was put up. When my brother got together with Della, they lived down at the mission at Turtle Point. That's where Lenny, her first, was born. We were still on the Clarence River then. Later, round about the 1950s when this mission over here was getting built, half the people was in it. Then Della and my brother, they got a house where Priscilla is now. He used to work for rations, do a little bit. Della used to work for rations, too. Della had about nine children then.

We'd go fishing. Sometimes we'd go horseriding. Della wasn't much of a horserider. Come home in the afternoon, then we'd go carrying wood from the timbers, cross the creek, we'd walk. That was for the open fire. Course in them days you didn't have cars or anything to get us wood. Only that horse and cart, and he wasn't much of a horse. That was before Della got pensioned and then they shifted to Bonalbo. Anyhow we shifted up there. I went up there and lived with them for a while. That's when my brother got sick.

That afternoon when my brother died when they took him to hospital, Della was raking up out the back. He had been out the back watching the children play. Della went inside and that's when he told her he was sick, a bit wonky. Little Della was only a baby when he passed away. When he died, she was only three months old. It was a sad time. Della had me, she had her biggest girl, Narelle, and she had Muriel to help with the washing and cooking and to clean the house. She took it hard for a long time.

Three months after he passed away, that's when John came up to Bonalbo. I stayed there then and looked after the kids. We helped rear them up to what they are today. Just to give her a bit of a break, you know. We used to tell her to go anywhere she wanted. So she used to go to Lismore or back down to her place at Maclean and Yamba or go to Baryulgil. We were just one big happy family. You see, Della used to have a big shed at the back of her place in Bonalbo. John and I, we lived in the shed. We used to have Della junior there. We had Susie, our own little one. Then we had Robyn and we had William—the little boy we call George Plus, we schooled all those boys of Della's. Them days it was really good old days, it was, you know.

We used to go up the gorge, Della and I and some of the boys, and look for porcupine round the hills. Then get melons, peaches, passionfruit. You know, if we didn't have anything in the house to eat for supper, the boys would go and get peaches and we'd boil them all up and we'd make custard. That'll go round a lot of people. Della also had a mulberry tree out the back there. John or Della would make a pie.

One day the boys were all playing. Douglas was the biggest, he ran that kangaroo down eh! At the swamp there, the kangaroo ran across the road and the boys chased it. They caught it and they killed it. They brought it back to us. Where I was staying in the white house—that's where the kangaroo ran straight across the road. Within five minutes that kangaroo was dead, oh true!

Della was one of those girls, them days you know, she wasn't a quick-tempered girl. She was full of fun, tell little stories and joke a lot. You'd hear all the women laughing. She was never angry or anything. She was just happy-go-lucky. In the afternoon when we'd come home, we'd all get together and she'd play marbles with us.

Cheating, she'd be cheating us. Take our marbles off us and everything! Before we could do anything, we had to do something for her before she would give us our marbles to play with.

Well, Della means a lot to me. She helped me, although she had her own children to rear, she helped me with mine when my first husband died. I had four children then and no-one to turn to. There was only Della and my brother to help me. That was before I married John. My mother died, then my father and then my husband. Della was the only one to comfort me. She was that sort of person. When I needed her, she was there. She was always there to give me a helping hand. That is why today I miss her, now she's left.

Recollections by the late John Laurie

When we used to stay down Plains Station there, Della was still a young girl. A farmer gave her a little pig. She called it Blacky. She nursed that pig till he was this big, till we sold him. They were the good old days when we used to work on dairy farms. We'd go fishing or go out bush walking, out to pick lemons and things like that. Tucker was cheap in those days.

When her husband died, you couldn't get her for a while to go out, you know, go around or anything. We used to help her with the kids at home and for a while after that, we reared them all up together. We looked after a lot of kids when we were young.

I grew up with Della and she means a lot to me. She done a lot for me since I came to Tabulam. I used to live with her and her husband, William. There was a lot of work around the bush and we used to work on the mines, Baryulgil asbestos mines. Come home, and Della would have everything ready for us. There was nothing we needed like, you know. She done a lot for me, my sister, and I appreciate it, what she done for me. I missed her when she went away to live.

Just mixing together

There were times when we just mixed together. These were always full of fun. Playing and laughing and joking with our mates. The mothers would often have a game with their kiddies. We'd play rounders and cricket and catching the ball—a bit of everything. Us mothers would be neck-a-neck with our children playing. I had some lovely friends, my mates up in Tabulam. We'd walk for miles and miles to go fishing or picking wild fruit—the lemons and oranges and peaches. We'd sit down on the side of the river bank and have a feed of the wild fruits while we fished. Dear, we enjoyed ourselves. Might catch about two or three catfish. Then we'd come home, clean them up and cook them for the kiddies' tea. The men, when they went hunting, used to shoot enough kangaroo to go around every home in the mission. We would share with one another the food that was caught in the bush.

We used to go prospecting for gold, any little amount. We thought we might hit it rich one day, find a reef and become rich, but that never happened. We did a lot of things together, my girlfriends and me. We'd go for firewood over to the other side of Black Creek and we'd sit down, looking back towards the mission telling stories and laughing. We'd look for porcupine underneath the logs. This was all a part of it. It was all fun to us.

Then when our children finished school we'd go back home. We'd make them change their clothes so that we could wash and iron them ready for the next day's school. The kiddies never used to give us any trouble. Some of the mothers would growl at their children. I used to say nasty things to mine too at times. Then I'd sit down and I'd think, 'Why did

I have all these children? Not to abuse around, not to go and say things that I shouldn't say. I should love them, and love them from the bottom of my heart.'

The women would go corn pulling or down to the Plains Station to pick gem peas and potatoes. All the women used to work together. We'd chip the weeds in the corn paddocks. I know what it's like to work in the paddocks like a man, just for a bit of bread or sugar and tea. We worked hard. When we'd get to the end of a row the women would sit for a spell and talk and joke and laugh. It was good to sit and be with your friends. We'd help each other to chip the weeds or maybe pull the corn and double bank it coming back along the rows. It was all fun. Well we thought it was fun, yet it was hard work, too. But it was something different from the housework. From the corn paddocks back into the house again. From the house we'd go over to the other side of the hills to get more wood for the fire. We used to carry wood a lot on our backs, across the creeks. The little boys would get the brambles of a morning. It was all fun though because I was a young woman in the spring of health.

One day we were looking for porcupine on the side of the hills. There was my two sisters-in-law, my niece and my other old mate. The others were up in front of me and I was walking along on my own by the creek and, blow me down, I walked straight into a porcupine! A big one it was. He was lying down curled up, must have just had a feed. You could see all his little tracks going round and round till they got to him, all curled up. It didn't take me long to kill him. I took him home and shared him up with the other mates.

We used to mix in together, my friends and me, but I had some arguments in my time, not only with women but with men, too. I stood toe-to-toe and argued with them. And they daren't hit me, they daren't, because they knew that I'd hit back. I wasn't the sort of person who wanted to be rowing with people all the time. I just corrected them and when I did they'd say to me, 'Why don't you mind your own business?' Well, I'd say, 'I can't mind me own business when you're already minding somebody else's.' But you know, as I say, life still goes on.

I've got a son called Billy. He was a great athlete at school. He'd win everything he went in for, everything. Even today he's still a great footballer. He played for the Canberra Raiders as a winger and I'm proud to be his mother. He's playing for the Clarence River now, down at Maclean. I hope that one day I'll see all my sons playing football. I've got about seven footballers now and I'm proud of the lot of them. They come from a football background. My father, my husband and my husband's father and his brothers, they were all good footballers.

This one special day, my Dad was playing down at Maclean. There used to be a big oval where they now have a carpark. Anyhow, this day Dad was playing football and my uncle was on the opposite team. Percy Creag his name was.

He was playing opposite to my father. Dad was full of speed and he was running that fast that when Uncle Percy grabbed him to stop him, he tore his thumb. Dad was just too fast. Uncle Percy's thumb was banging right off and he had to go up to the hospital to get it stitched back on.

Dad was a mighty man and this is how I see my sons today. If they put their minds to something they can do it. It's only putting your mind to things you think you can do. And when I say you can do it, you can, you can do it. And I'm a mother who loves and cares for her children. Well, I think all mothers do. It's good when you've got a big family, cause you've always got somewhere to go. You can always go to their homes, visiting them and they can always come to you. There's never a dull moment when you've got a big family. Christmas time you look forward to them coming home. You look for that little something that they've got for you. And it's the love. It's that love—they're reaching out for you and you've got to reach out to them. They'll put everything aside just to come and see you. Buy you little things just to show their appreciation to you as a mother.

My husband, he was a lovely man. William Walker was his name. He wasn't the sort of man to go around looking for a fight or an argument. He was a humble man, quiet and good. Somewhere down the line some things have just got to go wrong. You can't be perfect. You look around today, there's nobody perfect. We had our problems but I really loved my husband. I don't know, but when I first saw him, I just fell in love with him. I never bothered to look for any other man because he was the man I really did love deep down inside. I cared so much about him. He used to growl at the eldest boy. He'd get into him and say, 'Well stop this, stop doing that, stop doing this.' And the boy would say, 'I'm me own boss. I'm fifteen years of age.' My husband would say, 'No you're not, you're not your own boss.' But boys of that age, they think that they're their own boss. They want to be their own boss. There's so much we could teach our boys.

The eldest son of mine used to work down on the farm. They'd plough up the paddocks with the tractor. They thought that they were just it, taking it in turn to plough up the ground for the gardens on the farm. One year we had a lovely crop of corn. That was still in the days of managers. Each home was allowed to take so many cobs of corn at a time. Some families got more corn than the other families and they were told not to take any more. Well they wouldn't. Every one of the people on the reserve there at Tabulam, they did what they were told. If the manager told them not to do something, they wouldn't. The manager ended up selling the cattle and horses we had. I don't know who bought old Toby. That was the horse whose belly they were going to light a fire underneath.

I remember the first time I ever saw a baby delivered. It was my sister's. She got sick with her second son. Matron Levin, the manager's wife, came over. I didn't know anything about delivering babies so she told me to scrub my hands. I was so anxious I scrubbed my fingernails and everything till I was so clean. She showed me how to cut the cord, how to bring the afterbirth away. It was something. I was very proud to do, especially being my sister and my little nephew. It was so natural and beautiful to help bring that little life into the world. When he came out of his mother's womb and took the first breath of life, they turned him upside down and smacked him on the bum and he started to cry, opened his little lungs out. I wrapped him up then in a nappy and shawl and cuddled him. Then Matron Levin showed me how to deal with the mother. 'Get that afterbirth away, Della,' she said, 'you're doing pretty good.' It made me feel so good to know that I could do it.

About three weeks after that, this other girl took sick and there was no-one around. It was her first baby and the labour pains had started. We rang the ambulance but it couldn't make it in time. So, once again I had to do it. This time all alone I was a bit fidgety but I knew I could do it. I sterilised the scissors and had some clean binding and cloth ready. A beautiful little baby girl this time. The afterbirth came away nice and clean and I fixed the cord. Oh, I felt proud. Proud, because another little life had come into the world.

Many more I delivered over the years but the last one I delivered up at Tabulam was only a year or so ago. I was on the river bank fishing when my son came looking for me, about half past five in the evening. He was singing out, 'Mum, Mum where are you? Hey, Cathy's sick. She's gonna have her baby.' 'Wait on,' I called out. We jumped in the Land Cruiser and drove back into the mission. As I got there she had all these other girls around her. The pains were coming right on top of one another and the other girls didn't know what to do. Some of them were crying with her. So anyhow we got Bette Collins from over town, cause she was a nursing sister, to come and help. The ambulance driver landed just as the baby was born. So I delivered that little baby. It was premature, that one. We fixed her up and I said to Bette, 'Well Bette, there's no sense in keeping her here. Take her up there to Bonalbo.' So they took the mother and baby to Bonalbo and then rushed them straight to Lismore Hospital. It was a bit difficult for a while being premature and all, but now the baby's fine. She's in good health.

I feel so proud of myself for everything that I've done. I'm not skiting or anything, I'm just telling you what I did in the community. There were a lot of things that happened in the community. We used to go to these AFEC (Aboriginal Family Education Centre) meetings over at the old mission school house. Some Maoris came over from New Zealand to show us their way of teaching pre-schoolers. Mona Ramsay said to me, 'Della, if you want to teach your dialect to the younger ones, you must get them at this age, when they're first learning to talk. At this AFEC stage, pre-school stage, you must teach them.' Grannies, grandfathers, uncles and aunts who can speak the dialect, they go there and they speak it to them because at that age a child can pick it up so much quicker. That's what I say today, the younger ones in the preschools should be taught the dialect because it's dying out. The culture is dying out. All the Aboriginal ways are dying out on the North Coast as I see it. Too much *dagay* (white man) in our ways; *yirralee* (white or not good) ways, there's too much of it.

These days when you go into a shop you don't know what you're eating. It's all grease, most of the things are too fatty. As we get older we never stop to think about the food we eat and how to look after our bodies. How our bodies were once healthy. Why are we like this today? We're not eating the right food and we're not eating at the right times. We're not doing the things that we used to do years and years ago. As we get older we begin to run short of breath—too much car. Instead of walking to exercise our bodies we want to be driving around in cars. 'Oh, wait on I'll come with you, I can't walk.' This was all part of the exercise, how our old people used to one time go walkabout. Go hunting in the bush, getting out grubs. We call them *djubal,* white people call them witchetty grubs. Well, they're beautiful. Some time if you can get someone to show you how to cut the tree and get a feed of *djubal,* try it. It's beautiful and good to eat, full of protein.

We had a big Aboriginal day at Tabulam School. All the Aboriginal people came over from the reserve. The white people joined us. The hippies joined us. We all had a wonderful time. They all went out hunting and came back with *djubal,* white kids and all. We cooked them on the coals, we fried some, we grilled some—cooked them all ways. They couldn't get over how lovely they were. It's only just the thought that turns you off. You get a couple of nice big fat yellow *djubal* and try it. (Oh, I could have a nice feed of *djubal* now.) And kangaroo, slice a few pieces of kangaroo meat and roll it in flour or cook it on the coals. You can also mince it up. Put a bit of pepper and salt and onion with it and mince it all up, roll it up and cook it. Never wish for a better taste. It's something different.

Oh, I enjoyed the times when we would sit down and spin one another stories, joking around. You know, it's good when you've got a lot of friends around you, you're never lonely. When you've got your family around you, you're never lonely. And I like to be on the move. Cleaning up, washing, ironing, as long as I'm moving around, that's all that matters to me.

I'm glad that I'm the way I am. I care about everyone and I've got feelings for other people. I'd just like to say that I've got so many friends all over the place. I've got friends round about Australia. I've got friends overseas, even in America and all. I've got Christian friends. It's good to be recognised even though I'm an Aboriginal woman. It makes me feel good. When I was struggling to rear my family I had my brother and sister-in-law to help me. I had someone who cared, who always did care for me. And it's good to know. Most of all, I know there's someone greater who cares for me and gives me the strength to keep on going.

I just don't know what's going to happen to my people in years to come. We are fighting for land rights. Are we going to get the land? Some people have got their land, some haven't. But still and all, life goes on and we must go on. We mustn't row and fight with one another. Let's share Australia together. There's plenty of room for everyone. So why should us Aboriginal people and the non-Aboriginal people be greedy, why? When this land is so big and beautiful, let us all live together in it and share our love with one another, just mixing together.

Good times and sad times

We had sad times but we also had happy times. We used to go dancing a lot. Get all done up. Collected ochre paint from the rocks on the river bank. There were four different kinds that gave us red, yellow, cream and black. The rocks are smashed up till they're real fine, like baby powder. Then we'd do ourselves up. We thought we were just it because we had these ochre paints. We'd paint our lips and faces. You mix the dust up with a little bit of water then rub it on the lips with your finger. The cream one is very smooth when you grind it the right way, and we would rub this into our faces. You could feel how soft it was on your skin. All these things we had in the bush. You didn't have to go and buy them because they were there in the bush.

There was also what we called 'black gin's powder'. It's shaped like a mushroom but round and doesn't open out like a mushroom does. You rub that in for the complexion. It's very smooth and soft. Not so good to smell but very good for the skin. When it's first growing, it's white, then it goes brown and when it's ripe it turns black. A powdery sort of mushroom it is. That's all the old people used years ago for kiddies' chafe and things like that, was this powder. Very nice for the skin, put it on any part of the body.

Anyhow, we would get all done up and go to these dances. Everybody looked nice and lovely and slim. We'd take the kiddies along. They'd sleep up behind the stage. When we finished a dance we'd go up and have a peek to see if they were asleep or not. It was so much fun. We enjoyed ourselves, we did. Sometimes if there was no belle of the ball or special dance we would just have a dance for the fun of it.

I remember Aunty Marge, she was a big woman but very light on her feet. Her and Alma Wilson, they were both very light. They'd do the mazurka and all the different dances. How they used to jump! It was wonderful to watch. And the partner that Aunty Marge had, he was a thin man, tall and thin. There was Aunty Marge with a little short dress but she looked so nice. Oh, she was light on her feet. I never saw a dancer like her. When she used to swing around she would swing on her toes. Aunty Alma was the same I'd sit down and just watch them dance.

There'd always be a big feed, big supper. There was everything there—wild food and things that we baked. The big tables would be set and we'd go and help ourselves. Wasn't much to get into the hall either, as long as they got something. But oh, it was fun, that's the beauty part of it. Today they think that they can't go without beer or some sort of alcohol to have a party or a dance. We never bothered with it those days, as long as we had fun.

There's so much I could talk about, things that happened in those days. It was funny how some of the older chaps used to put black boot polish on their hair to hide the grey. When they got hot and started to sweat the polish would begin to melt. You'd see these black streaks trickling down their faces as they danced. They didn't know. They thought when the young girls giggled that they were giggling at them dancing. They'd put it on their eyebrows and all. Then when they'd wipe the sweat off with a hanky or rag, the black polish would go all over their faces looked so funny. I can still see it now.

I used to take all the younger kiddies to the dances. My little boys Cedric and Douglas, and Bella Anne, they all used to come. Course everyone wanted to go to the dances, everyone. We used to jitterbug. It was the latest dance in those days.

We'd twist our bones around. I was a bit of a rocker. Now days I'm lucky to wobble cause I'm so big. Before I'd finished having my family I was nice and slim. When I think of the old days I can still see them fellas swinging around with the boot polish running down their faces.

I remember one very big ball we had down at Yamba, people came from all over. I was only about eleven at the time. Aunty Elsie didn't have anything to wear to this ball so this white woman she worked for lent her a dress. 'Oh Elsie, you don't have to buy a dress. I've got one you can wear,' she said. 'Oh, thank you missus,' Elsie said. She was so grateful. She got the dress and went down and had her bath. She wanted to try it on before the dance, so she slipped it over her body and as she went to pull it down it started to tear. The dress was that old it just fell apart. 'Oh goodness gracious me,' she said. 'What kind of woman is she? I gotta go and see this woman. I'll tell her, I'll get into her, fancy giving me a dress like this!' Finally she got a dress. My sister gave her a lovely dress to wear and she went and did herself up for the ball, put the boot polish into her grey hairs and all.

Talking again about the dances we had up in Tabulam, there was a violin player, an accordion player, sometimes we'd have a mouth organ and of course the spoons. That was our band and we danced to their tunes. It was just great that we could get out and swing our legs around the floor. Some people would do the waltz, some would do other kinds of dances, some of them didn't know how to dance at all. They would go putting the wrong foot in the wrong place but they didn't care just as long as they were moving around that floor.

One time Mr Soorley, the teacher, and his wife were there doing a different kind of dance. Of course it was the white fella's way. We all stopped. We were watching them dance. We thought, 'Hello, this is a new dance.' While some of us were doing the old dance they were doing it in a different way. But the thing is we enjoyed ourselves, we all had a good time. Weren't allowed to have any alcohol so there was no-one there to muck the dance up. No-one to row around or upset the dance. It was good for us all to get together and enjoy ourselves. When it was time for the dance to finish the manager would come along and point to his watch for us all to go. We'd go home happy If we didn't leave as soon as the manager said, he would call the police. He was that strict.

At Christmas time we'd have a party on the reserve. Every child used to get a present. Course the presents those days were very cheap, not like today. Us mothers enjoyed ourselves because we knew it was just getting together having a party with our kiddies. To see their little faces light up, how their little hearts were overjoyed when they'd see the table spread with all these lollies and biscuits and cakes and sandwiches. Everything we used to have, there was soft drink and ice-cream, everything for everybody.

My husband was still at the asbestos mines working. When he'd come home of a weekend he'd go working with his white mates in town, but then again it was only for half a day and he'd come home and have the rest of the day with us. He wasn't working to come home drunk and scatter us around. He'd work really hard for the food.

We lived at Bonalbo for a while, then I had my last baby. After having thirteen babies in the missions, I had my last baby. There was Lenny, Narelle, John, Ricky, Billy, Cedric, Douglas, Bella Anne, Rocky, Phillip, Raymond, Lewis and the little daughter who died. I called the new baby girl Della, my little namesake. I gave her three names, Della Adelaide Marie Walker She was born on the 4 March 1971. That's the same year my husband died. He died on the 9 June, my husband.

This left me all alone with my family. I was alone and it was a struggle. I battled to raise those kiddies. Doing all their washing by hand and their ironing. I had one of those old irons you heat on the fuel stove. With all the other work that needed doing it was a struggle for me. I've been so grateful to John and Adelaide all these years because if I ever wanted to go anywhere they would stay home and watch the little ones for me. They helped me rear my children in my time of need. They played a big part because I was just a lonely mother with the father gone and our little daughter gone. I was just a lonely mother.

Sometimes I used to sit down and cry. Deep down inside me I used to cry, day and night. In the mornings and just as the sun was getting ready to go down, they're the times I felt it most. I'd get down and I'd cry to myself, 'Why did this happen to me? Why did you leave me with all this family?' You see, just before he died he got sick.

Well, I was raking up the backyard and he was playing with little Ricky and Douglas and Bella, lighting crackers and throwing them up in the air. All of a sudden he got up and went inside. Ricky followed him in and then he came back outside and said to me, 'Mummy, Daddy want you.' So anyhow, just as the sun was going down, this must have been the time when the pains were getting worse. When I went in he was leaning over the bed. He was in a cold sweat and in terrible pain. He said to me, 'I don't know what's wrong but I'm getting these terrible pains.' I asked him where and he said, 'On the back and in the stomach.' I tried to rub it to ease the pain but it didn't seem to help. He started getting worse so I sent one of the kids up to Doug Walden who was a painter friend in Bonalbo. I told my husband that I'd get him to a doctor and that I'd come with him. We had no time to get cleaned up or anything. Mr Walden came down with his car and away we went. 'What's wrong Billy?' he said. 'Oh, I'm getting terrible pains.' He was all in a sweat.

We rushed him up to the doctor. I said, 'Please, I've bought my husband up to see you, he's very sick.' The doctor said, 'Go somewhere else. I don't want to see him. Take him to Casino where he always goes. He hasn't been back here so take him away.' And he started abusing us, using terrible disgusting swear words. He started saying these terrible words. On the way back to the car I said, 'Well would you ring the ambulance?' He said, 'I'm not ringing no ambulance, you take him.'

I had a car there at my place but I couldn't take him to Casino because I didn't have a licence. Mr Walden couldn't take him because he wasn't a well man himself and Casino was a long way away. Someone managed to ring an ambulance for him and it arrived later that night. On the way to the hospital there was a message waiting at the Mallanganee Range tick gate for it to turn back and pick up baby twins from the reserve at Tabulam. I couldn't go with him because I had the little ones to see to. I don't know what time they finally got him to the hospital but at seven o'clock the next morning they transferred him to the Base Hospital at Lismore. All that night he lay in Casino with the aches and the pains.

As soon as he got to Lismore they operated on him. We rang up at eight o'clock and they told us to ring back at ten. We rang back and they told us the operation was a success. My eldest daughter Narelle rang. She was running down the road, yelling, 'Mummy he's good, Daddy's good.' It filled my heart with joy to know that he was alright. About an hour and a half later the police came and told me I was wanted at the hospital straight away. I didn't know anything, didn't know what was going on.

We rang the two eldest boys who were working at Baryulgil and they came home. I had the car there so we went on to Lismore. I didn't know my husband was dead till we got to the hospital, didn't know nothing. My sister-in-law in Baryulgil, Susan Donnelly, she knew before I did. We got there late in the evening. My brother and sister-in-law and the bigger kids, we all went down to see him. When we got there the nurse said, 'Oh just a minute I'll ring for the doctor to come and see you.' I started to think, you know, but still not realising there was anything wrong. The doctor finally came. He was about ten minutes, I suppose. He asked, who was Mrs Walker. I said, 'I'm Mrs Walker.' He came over to me and put his arm on my shoulder and he said, 'I'm sorry Mrs Walker, we did everything we could for your husband. The operation was a success but the old heart failed him, the heart just couldn't take it.'

Well, if there was a hole in that hospital I'd have went straight through. That's the way I felt. I just couldn't believe it, I just couldn't. They asked us if we'd like to come and see the body. They took us into the ward where he was lying down. There was a screen around him. I walked in and looking at him, you'd swear he was sound asleep. There were no wrinkles in his face, nothing. He looked like he was in a deep sleep. I just couldn't believe my eyes. I felt all alone. I felt lonely, there were the children to think about. I didn't know what to do.

We had the funeral and it was all over but I still had the loneliness for months and months. Inside me that loneliness was still there. What that doctor at Bonalbo said to me, it's still in the back of my mind, it's still there. A chap that could come out and use dirty swear words like that, that's the kind of doctor he was. I had to live with all that inside of me. I was too frightened to talk to any white people about it because he was their doctor too. You know, deep down inside me, I feel there was some discrimination there from that doctor for my family. Later on my son John, he had a car accident I was in Yamba at the time. My eldest son Lenny and another chap took him up to that doctor. 'Oh I don't want to see him, take him somewhere else.' He ended up treating him because Casino was a good hour away but he said, 'I can't have him in this hospital too long.' We had to live like that all those years.

Life wasn't easy for me but I had to go on. I had to go and work, to be doing something to get it out of my mind. I tried never to stop and think too much. I just wanted to think about the good times. The minute I started thinking about sad times I got up and kept myself busy, doing something, moving about. I didn't go to parties to rid myself of the worry, but I went to church and I started to get involved.

Recollections by Maggie Olesen

Della wasn't the first member of her family I met when I moved to Bonalbo in 1977 I first met her daughters. There was Bella. I used to call her 'Bella Bellissima'. She was in high school at that time, and there was little Della who was just about ready to start school. She was about six years old and an absolute little doll. And, of course, the way children are whenever there's a newcomer in the village, the children flock to see them and see who they are and what they're doing. So the children would flock to my house, you see, with their friends and it was through them that I came to know Della.

Della is a very handsome Aboriginal woman, obviously the matriarch of the village. Whenever any one of the Aborigines had any sort of problem they would go to Della's house. Della's sister-in-law, Adelaide, lived next door to her. And I should say that at any time you would be likely to find up to perhaps two dozen people living in the two houses, because anyone who was in trouble used to go there. Not only that but they used to go there because it was lovely to be with Della who's a very warm, outgoing person. I didn't find it so easy to meet the Aboriginal adults as I found it to meet the Aboriginal children. In fact, the little boys used to come to my house and say, 'Please Maggie, may we cook witchetty grubs in your house because nobody else will let us!' And I used to say, 'Right, you can come in but only provided you cook the grubs with garlic and butter.' And so they used to do that and it was all very delicious and we had very good times indeed.

Once a week the Uniting Church held Aboriginal services. These services were absolutely tremendous. The services of the European community in Bonalbo tend to be rather staid affairs. Not very many people going to them, perhaps a dozen, perhaps less, in the church at any time, but the Uniting Church on Wednesday was absolutely crowded out. The music thundered out with the drums and guitars playing and, of course, all the children and adults singing at the tops of their voices and clapping and dancing. Their services always followed the same sort of pattern. First of all they would have choruses. Then interspersed with the choruses, they would have testimonies of what had happened during the week and everybody, sometimes even the children as well, would pop up and make their testimony—some way that they had been helped or some problem that they had.

Later on, the services moved to Lismore rather than Bonalbo Uniting Church. Harry Walker was appointed as pastor of the Aboriginal Church of Lismore. I saw rather less of Della. Her children were growing up and also Della was wandering around—no, 'wandering' is the wrong word—Della was visiting around the country. After that, Della could hardly stay in the same place. She was always moving about. She has a huge collection of friends and one of the things that is very important to Della is that she has contact with her friends all over the place, and they need her too.

It was at that time, there was a little bit of trouble in the Bonalbo school because the Aboriginal and white children were not getting on very well. The headmaster decided that he would really try hard to do something to bring the two races together and so he invited the Aborigines to become counsellors of the school and to come and talk to them about the problems they found and discuss these problems with him. Della became one of those counsellors. After that, the school developed very strong associations with the Aboriginal community, so much so, that the Bonalbo School is now quite a pioneer in Aboriginal studies, which the white children attend and experience as well as the Aboriginal children. They do quite a bit of dancing. They learn about the Aboriginal way of life and how they can live in the bush looking for plants and the food that Aborigines find in the bush. They really are learning together quite a lot of the Aboriginal culture.

One of the things I think Europeans find difficult to understand is, they talk for instance about the spiritual affinity for the land and the Aborigines, but what we don't understand is that the land is the

Aborigines' botany. It is their zoology. It is their library. It is their reference book. All the things that we've got in the libraries, all the knowledge we've got in libraries is there. It is their geography. All the culture that we have in books and knowledge, it is there, localised in the land. And once the land is taken away from them, all their complete culture goes because it is so fixated in the actual landmarks. Their legends are in the land. They weren't written in books. They are in the land itself.

Almost twelve years have passed since I first knew Della. Della has aged, and has aged magnificently. She really is a proud queen walking the roads of Australia. She has got diabetes now and recently she injured her foot. Despite anything anybody could do, Della would not go into hospital. In the end, I believe that her relatives literally had to kidnap her and take her to the hospital where she was very ill for quite some time. But she is now out of hospital and I understand that she has gone walkabout again. She is an indomitable character. May she travel the roads of Australia for many, many years to come.

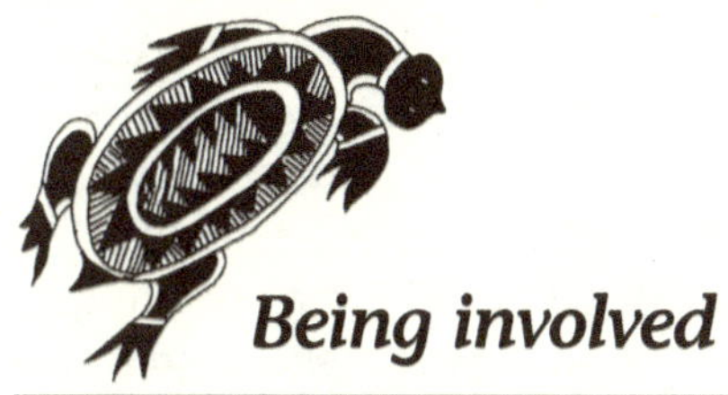

Being involved

When I got involved in the church we would travel all over the place for gospel meetings. We had a church in Bonalbo. They used to let us have the Uniting Church building. Aboriginal people from all parts would come. We had special nights when we would go to church for worship and enjoy one another's testimony. We would share the things that had happened to us. I've seen a lot of miracles in that little church in Bonalbo.

My friend Maggie Olesen is a wonderful lady. She would come down and enjoy the fellowship we had with our brothers and sisters from far and near. We'd have a prayer to open up the meeting and then we'd sing our opening hymn,

There's a land that is fairer than day,
And by faith we can see it afar,
For the Father waits over the way,
To prepare us a dwelling place there
In the sweet by and by we shall meet on that beautiful shore

You know, when we sang that you could see the tears rushing down our sisters' and brothers' faces. You'd see the smiles and the glory of the Lord all around us.

We would offer prayers for certain things or certain people. Many people would come out for prayer and the presence, the spirit of the Lord would lay them on the floor. It feels so beautiful because you know you're not in there alone. It's not a boring time when you get sick of sitting down and listening to the preaching, it's joyful.

Maggie came one day to ask for prayer for this awful head cold that she had. We put our hands on her head and asked

God to take the cold from her body, to take it away. Well, the spirit of the Lord it sent her on the floor and the cold was gone. When the people come out for prayer they get up from the floor like they are staggering but it is the Lord claiming their spirit. I saw this happen to different ones. There was this little boy with a crippled foot and he had a special shoe. Today that little boy is walking and his foot is as straight as anything.

I am a great believer in the word of God. Many times things have almost happened. One time we were driving from Maclean to Tabulam in my car and the girl that was driving didn't know the road. I was in the front seat with her and she was driving. Well, she took this turn too wide. She came too far out. When she went to hit the brakes the car slid. It must have slid about fifty yards and ended up right on the edge of this big embankment. We could have gone over that embankment and I wouldn't be here today to tell you this story.

There's another girl up at Tabulam today. She's now twenty-one years of age. When she was a little one of about four or five she couldn't even crawl. Her mother, a young niece of mine, took her back and forwards to the doctor. He said she had no hip socket. One night she brought the daughter up to church. Pastor Eddie Hickling was there. She brought that little one out for prayer and he anointed her head with oil and prayed for her. Believe it or not but God gave her a brand new socket. The mother used to put a tic (mattress) on the floor beside the bed in case she ever fell but that morning after the prayer, the mother came in and the girl was standing up on the tic. The mother didn't know what to do. She just looked at her girl and started to cry. God has filled that mother's heart with joy to see her little girl standing up. A girl that the doctor said would never walk. We thank God for that. He is the God of the universe and He saves and keeps and satisfies. He understands our ways and we must learn to understand His too, you know, because He gives and takes.

I had a son who was an alcoholic. I'd say to him, 'Don't drink any more, son.' He just went on drinking and drinking

and he died. I was a mother broken-hearted. I'd already lost a daughter. I'd lost my husband. Now I had to lose a son. To me it was something that I had to go through in my Christian walk of life. I couldn't understand why this had to happen. My son wouldn't take any notice of me. He'd say, 'No Mummy, I will never drink again, never.' Yet, he couldn't stop.

I just thank God today for the health and the strength He has given me to go on. As I go on with life I try to push the past aside but it's something you can't push aside. The memories live on. Sometimes I wonder what would have happened had he still been alive today. That's all I can do now, is live day-to-day. If I wasn't a Christian woman I'd have been in a mental home with all the worries and struggles I've had in life. It's lovely to have a Saviour that you can look to. You know He's there with you. When the Lord is with you, you can feel the presence. It's a different feeling, not human but spiritual.

Not long after my eldest son died I had to go into hospital to get a toe amputated. I've got sugar diabetes. Through my foolishness, through me not doing the right thing, this is what happened. I knew I was going into theatre on this certain Tuesday morning. When they were leading me into the theatre all the fear left me. It just went away. I said to the nurse, 'I'm not frightened any more of going into theatre All the fear, it's gone.' I'd never been into theatre before. I was asking God to be with me and guide me. I went in there and when I came to, I went straight up for visiting hour. Different ones said to me, 'How do you feel love?' I said, 'Oh, I feel good.'

The second time was about a week later. I had to go in to get the foot all stitched up. This time when they wheeled me in and the doors closed behind me I felt all locked in. You see, it was the same theatre my poor son had died in and this was in my mind. I felt hopeless, there was nothing I could do. So I whispered a little prayer. I said, 'Lord you said in your word that you would never leave me nor forsake me, so guide me and see me through this and with your covering of the blood be with me, my heavenly father.' So it was just like going in and coming out again. It was a feeling that I never had before. I could smell this human blood and I felt there was no hope. The doctor came in and gave me the needle to put me to sleep. I didn't know anything then till it was all done. And I thank God for the breath of life.

Although I didn't have any education I also got involved with the schools. I knocked myself off in third class because I thought education was nothing. So, after all this time I began doing things at the schools. I got involved with the Djunagun Dance Troupe, taking them around to different places for performances. I'd go into the schools with the elders, Eric and Unis Walker to speak Bundjalung. The kiddies loved the Aboriginal Bundjalung dialect. We'd teach them the different parts of the body, certain parts of the face and the hair. After we were there a couple of times, the kiddies, even the white ones, they knew what we meant. They had the answers and there were some good little students in the school. This is Tabulam School I'm talking about. I'd point to the nose and they'd say *muru*. Your eyes, they are *geyo*. The ear is *binang*, and *jinung* is the foot. I loved going to the schools. I did it a lot.

In those days when I started to travel around I also got involved in community work, doing things to keep my mind occupied. Different things in different ways. I got involved in land rights. We went to Sydney and marched with another lot of Aboriginal people. In 1968, I remember I was at one march. We were just about at the end and my aunty was in a car with the Aboriginal queen of the march, waving to the crowd. They were ahead of us and as we were entering the gates to go into this, like a park it was, I could hear these Italians and they were singing out, 'Hooray for the Aborigines.' They started to clap us. It made me feel that we were something, it uplifted me. I know inside of me I had that feeling I can't explain it but it was really something when they sang, 'Hooray for the Australian Aborigines.' We marched through the gates and stayed there for a while. We were all billeted out to different homes so after a cup of tea we went our own way.

It was good going around meeting different people. Once I even ended up in Canberra. Eric and Unis Walker and myself went down there and met Neville Wran (the Premier of New South Wales at that time). We talked to a lot of white politicians. We passed through Bega and Nowra, all the towns along the way, talking to the people. Sometimes we'd have little church meetings. It was lovely. Most important of all, it was meeting with our own people, listening to their points of view and listening to the stories they told us about the old days and how hard it was. We went to a place on the South Coast where these five boys were killed in a car accident. We were there at the time it happened. It was very sad to see our people at that time. We worked our way down to Canberra, stopping a week or two wherever there were fruit or vegetables that needed picking. This gave us our petrol money. It was good because as we went along we were able to exchange ideas with other Aboriginal people in different communities. We made friends with a lot of people and saw a lot of places.

It's wonderful when you get with a group of people and they're talking about the land, our land. We're lucky to get a little piece of ground. We're not asking for much. In the beginning it was ours anyhow. All this buying and selling, it's hard for us to understand. In the old days our people never abused the land. They only took enough for their needs. No-one had more than anyone else and everybody was happy. Even if I could get a piece of land for the boys to plough up so I could grow vegetables, that we could have something of our own, not something that belongs to someone else. Something of our own where I could hold my head up and say, 'This is mine, this is for my family, this is ours.' That's all I've got left now, is my family.

The second time I went to Canberra I was involved in a march for land rights. Charlie Perkins, Owen Anderson and myself with some other people from other Aboriginal organisations led the students across the bridge. Marched with our heads up in the air for land rights, right to the park not far from Parliament House. This was the first time for me to see Parliament House. We were on the lawns and some reporters came up to me and asked if I'd like to say something to be on the news, so I did.

For me, coming from the bush like I did to the big city and bright lights, it was like coming from a place that didn't exist. But for me it was lovely to be able to speak to the news people. I spoke about the land. How much land there was up at Tabulam, what we wanted to do for the people. It was good seeing different people, all the different Aboriginal people. There were some full bloods from way up north. I listened to them tell about their land and what they wanted to do with it. We were all there to talk about the land.

Charlie Perkins was a lovely man. After the march we went to his place. He invited us around for a barbecue and a sing song. We sang, 'There's a Land That Is Fairer Than Day'. We sang that song and Charlie Perkins was overjoyed to have Aboriginal people from a different part of Australia in his backyard. He's also got a lovely wife, he's a well-spoken man and he's come a long way. What he spoke for, what he said, he said in a strong voice. He was a man of honesty. I thought he was a real gentleman. Now I'm getting on in age but I was there with the best of them, even politicians. I was in everything. I played a big part in the community and I worked hard in those days.

One time I'd like to tell you about is my trip to Alice Springs. I was in the aeroplane flying over the Simpson Desert. Looking down at the desert I was thinking, 'Fancy walking across that.' *If* you had a car and it broke down you wouldn't be able to see a house. There were no houses, just sand and little trees, the trees looked so tiny. There was nothing else there. When we got to Alice Springs everything was so dry. There was no green grass. The trees had a bit of green on them but the ground was bare and dry.

As we were driving into town from the airport we met a mob of Aborigines. We stopped and shook hands with them and had a talk. This was two or three miles out of Alice Springs which is a lovely little town and goodness gracious me, nearly every second person was Aboriginal. They took us out to the place we were staying. We had to clean it up ourselves. We took our own things to lay on. I brought a big quilt with me and I bought a new sheet from the shops. Just as well it was hot over there because that's all I had. But I enjoyed myself because again it was meeting Aboriginal people from all over Australia. It was a big education get-together we were at, like a conference. We met in little groups for discussions then went back into the big meetings. I talked about the things we did back home and about our language and ways of setting up systems to pass the knowledge on.

One night they had this great big barbecue for us. There was one Chinese fella there and he wanted to learn the lingo too. Some local girls came out and had a dance. This Chinese fella got up and he started to dance with the young Aboriginal girls. Dear, he enjoyed himself.

There was a little busload of Islanders and they sang a song in their dialect, swaying their bodies in time to the beat. It was so beautiful. There were some white women from a university in Sydney, Margaret Sharpe was there from way up in Armidale, Bob Morgan and some Aboriginal women from Sydney that are involved in education were there too. We all enjoyed ourselves singing and dancing by the light of the big fires. It was something new to us to get out over there, right in the centre of Australia. Who'd ever think that I'd go there.

When we were ready to go home we were waiting in this park for our ride. We saw all these boys. They had a big cassette player. First time I ever saw this done. I could see these boys dancing and twisting their bodies round and round. I said to my mate, 'What they doing over there?' She said, 'That's rap dancing.' I was thinking, 'Oh gee, they're raps doing that dance.' You'd see one coming out from one corner twisting his body, then you'd see another fella coming out from another comer twisting his body. They'd go back and another lot would come out from a different comer. I'd never seen anything like it but they sure drew the attention. There was a big crowd watching them in the park. They danced and danced and danced. I thought, 'By Jove, just look at these boys.' Then they danced upside down on their heads and tried to swing their bodies around in the air I thought, 'Gee whizz, it's a wonder they don't hurt themselves, the silly boys.' But to them, I suppose it was a dance. To me it was a silly dance. Young people today, they'll enjoy themselves with any dance. They wouldn't care I just looked at them in wonder.

While we were in Alice Springs, a mate of ours had gone to Uluru (Ayers Rock). It was about seventy miles out. He said it was so beautiful. We were not far away, and to think that we couldn't get there. This other chap said to me, 'If we'd have known you wanted to go to Ayers Rock we might have arranged something earlier.' When our mate came back and started telling us about it, oh, how we wished we were there I suppose it just wasn't my time to go.

We finished the trip to Alice Springs and away we came back home. We caught the aeroplane to Brisbane. A funny thing happened when I was up in the air. We left Alice about four in the afternoon and as we passed over the Simpson Desert I could see this blackness coming. I was watching out the window and thinking to myself, 'Now what's that?' You see, when we left Alice it was still bright, the sun was up high but when we passed over the desert and came towards Brisbane it was going down and darkness was coming I was thinking, 'Good gracious, what's going wrong? What's going to happen to us?'

The girl on the plane must have been watching me because she came to me then and asked if I was alright. I said, 'Yes I'm alright, thanks,' so she went back again. Just as we were coming into Brisbane for touchdown my ears started to go funny. She came to me again and said, 'Are you alright?' I said, 'Look love, I'm having trouble with my ears. I've got a buzzing sound in them! 'Oh well,' she said, 'I'll give you something for it! She gave me a tablet and sat down alongside me then. After a while she asked me how I felt I said, 'Oh, I feel real good now.' I'd taken that tablet, you see.

When we landed in Brisbane we went along to the place we were booked into and left for home the following day. I spent a couple of nights in Lismore with my sister, then I went home to my family. We had a lovely trip. It was good to meet all different kinds of Aboriginal people. There's not only one type of Aboriginal people, there's many different kinds—with different languages and things like that. When one Aboriginal person does anything wrong they seem to paint us all with the same brush like we're all the same, but we're not all the same. We have different types of people just like the white people. There are different classes of white people and so you have the same with the Aboriginal people of Australia.

It was good to get back home to my family but I'll always be grateful that I have been able to travel. I've been all around. I used to like going out to Moree. I'd go chipping cotton, stay with friends out there and chip cotton for a few weeks then come home again. We'd call into Tingah and Inverell and have a couple of nights there for church on the way back to Tabulam. When I think about those times I remember them as good. I had to go somewhere to stop me from thinking about my old memories of my husband who's gone. I had to get out and meet the people. I had to go and see the different places for myself. I met people from around the world and wherever there was a big church rally we would move on. I enjoyed myself and today I still want to enjoy myself.

When I was young I was frightened. I was shy until I started going into the schools and talking with the white teachers. I found that I could hold my head up high and talk and do things with them, be a part of what was going on. One time I couldn't mix. It was hard but I did it at last. I did it and I found out that I could relate to a white person. I am just as good as what the white woman is. Although they might have had a better education, although they might have had a better home, although they come from a better class of family,

I am what I am and I can't change that.

This is most important, that we should never think that we are nothing or nobody. We are all human beings, we are the people. It's good that our children can go to mixed schools and be involved in sports and things. This is everything to our people—mixing, sharing, caring for one another. That's why it's so important for our Aboriginal people to mix. Not to downgrade themselves but to mix with the white people. For our children to go to school with their heads in the air. They've got the same brains as white people.

I'm grateful that I could go into the schools and tell my white friends, the teachers, about the old times and things that have happened in my life. To do this without being ashamed of myself or putting myself down. I could stand up tall and say, 'I am not afraid.' I've got nothing to be ashamed of and this is all I live for today, that I can tell the people about the old times, about things that really did happen. It's good to be able to breathe in the freshness and feel free, to be able to go out into the community among my white friends and feel proud. I am a proud Aboriginal woman!

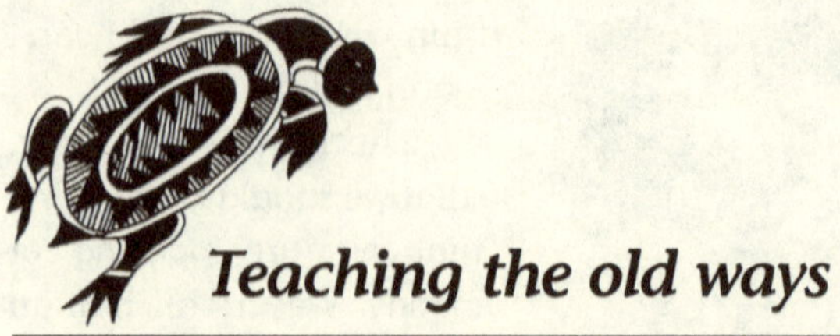

Teaching the old ways

When I came back from touring around I settled back in at home. That's when I started getting involved with the College of Advanced Education at Lismore. I was on the Aboriginal Council. We'd talk about the needs of our people in the area and discuss why things weren't working or what could be done, especially in relation to the schools. Then I would go back to Tabulam and talk things over with the community. We had a representative on the council from each area. Our job then was to go back to our own areas and get the community involved. This was good because it made people realise all the things that needed to be done.

Of course we spoke about funding for different things, mainly Aboriginal art in the schools. We also had a sewing class for the women at the reserve. They'd teach the young girls and us oldies too, how to sew. Then another lady came from the college and taught us all this secretarial business. How to do the books and accounts, all these bits and pieces that we wanted to learn. The women were good enough to come and teach us. We got a lot of things going in the community and they're still happening now.

I was eager to learn, to be taught and to be able to grasp things. I wanted to grasp every little thing I could that was concerned with learning. That's why I encourage the young ones today to go on with their education, particularly my own boys. They used to muck up at school certainly, but still and all, I tried to encourage them to go on. One of my sons spent a few months at the college at Grafton learning bookkeeping and things. He didn't stick out the whole course but the thing is he gave it a go. Now he knows enough not to let himself be done over. One of my other sons, Cedric, is at this moment attending college in South Australia. He's very forward and eager to learn more about our people.

If a child can't grasp the learning in books, as sometimes happens, they should be encouraged in things they are good at. All my children are good at sports. All the way through school they were always going around to different sporting events—football, basketball and netball. When the time would come for them to play a big match they'd get all teed up for it. I would get all excited too. It was good for me to be able to go along and be a part of my kiddies' sport. If you can involve yourself in your kids' education, doesn't matter how, it can only be good for them.

It is good that your voice can be heard. It is important to us that our kids benefit by what we do. As I work in the community I try to get people to understand my ways as an uneducated Aboriginal woman and, of course, it enables me to understand the ways of others. I also spend a lot of time going to the schools and telling the children about the old ways. I would tell them dreamtime stories of how the Clarence River was made. This is one of the stories I tell to them.

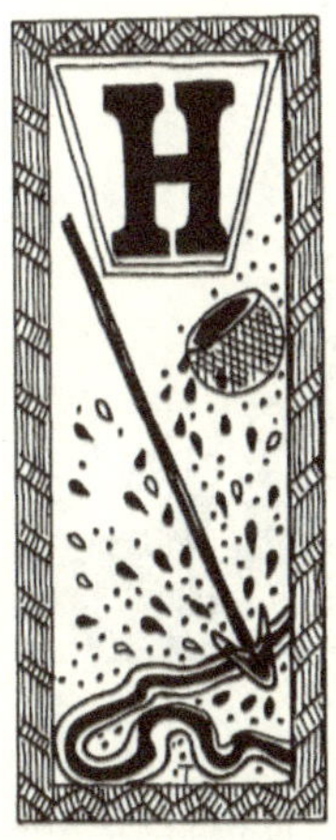

How the old woman, the old Dirrangun, how bad she was to her Balugan, a nice handsome young man. She was a wicked woman and very cruel. She even planted (hid) the water away from this Balugan so she could have it all to herself. She covered the waterhole with bladey grass and bark. Now when the Balugan started to get thirsty, he noticed there was no drinking water about and he suspected his old mother-in-law had stolen it for herself.

He set off with his two hunting dogs to find the water. The dogs scared a big *guruman* (kangaroo) and ran off after it. When the Balugan called his dogs back he saw that they had water dripping from the hair on their mouths. He followed the dogs until they led him to the waterhole. Then he started to clear it, pushed the bladey grass and bark away. He was all worked up and savage, so he stuck his *bilal* (spear) in the mountain releasing all the water.

The old woman was trying to block the water. The Balugan called out to her, 'You must be punished for your selfishness old woman, let the water you stole wash you away from this place.' The water gushed out of the hills, and streams started to flow over the rocks. Dirrangun was swept away but she fought bravely against the river. She spread her legs against the current but the water swept on to become creeks. The old woman was washed right down to Yamba. The Balugan turned her into a *budjegar* (fig tree). If you row down to Yamba you might still see the old Dirrangun waving her branches as you pass by.

Balugan releasing the water to form the Clarence River. Drawing by Lewis Walker.

The children looked forward to me going into the schools and telling about the dreamtime and all the old Aboriginal culture. The teachers, myself and the kiddies would all go hunting for the wild honey or the *djubal* (witchetty grub) and I'd tell them about the bush I used to show them how to make damper on an open fire. At Tabulam during Aboriginal Week we caught and cooked bush food. One year, one of my sons found a nice big porcupine and I cleaned him up and baked it along with a couple of big dampers. We took them to the school in the morning and everyone went *djubal* hunting. Oh, they got lots of big juicy *djubal* from beneath the wattle trees. Then we went back to school and had a big feed with the porcupine and kangaroo and we cooked the *djubal* there on the coals. Gertie Robinson made up a whole lot of scones on the fire with the kiddies. How the white people enjoyed it. They couldn't help eating it. They said, 'My, my, this is a lovely feed.' They just couldn't get over it. It's all clean food. It's not dirty because they only eat grass and wood anyhow. You'd never starve while you're out in the bush because there are all these things you can feed off. (My mouth's watering now just telling you about it.) It's so good when you go out in the bush to smell the fragrance of the bush. It's the wildness and it's wonderful to be able to inhale the beauty, you know, God's beauty.

A good friend of mine, Elizabeth Torrens, and myself would go over to the pre-school at Tabulam and the kiddies would come and sit under the big fig tree at home cause I lived next door there for a while. We'd tell the dreamtime stories and we'd teach them our dialect. All the parts of the face and body we'd teach them 'What's this?' we'd say pointing to the mouth. *'Tan,'* they'd say. Our teeth are *dirang* and the face, well this is our *mibihn*. The kiddies were so anxious, they wanted to learn things. My, oh my, we enjoyed ourselves.

One little white boy, Bradley Laurie, every morning he would stand up and sing me a song "Twinkle twinkle little star how I wonder what you are'. And he was so serious, he'd roll his little eyes around. He was a lovely student. The white kiddies were very interested, but our own little kiddies, the black kiddies, they didn't give two hoots about the dialect. They'd be climbing up the trees, but the white boys and girls were so eager to learn the dialect and about our ways. After the lesson I'd cook some johnny cakes on a gridiron over the ashes. They didn't just have one piece, they'd have two or three. It was so much fun for them.

Of course I wasn't doing it for the money. It was voluntary and I did it for the kiddies. I wanted them to achieve something. Now today the pre-school has two Aboriginal teachers and a white teachers' aide. How the white kiddies relate to the Aboriginal kiddies and to the Aboriginal teachers, it's really something. That's what we've got to do, learn to mix. The more we mix the better off well be. Instead of having the feeling that you don't like someone because they're not the same colour, we've got to learn to live together. I wasn't reared to have any hatred against the white people. As I said before, were all human beings.

Just before I left Tabulam to come back to Maclean I was administrator at the Tabulam Mission, I was president of the Housing Company and president of the Lands Council. We worked hard but the thing is we worked side-by-side. Today, I can see the results of all that hard work. Whatever decisions were made they were stuck to. You've got to be firm, no fighting, no arguing. They've just finished building five new units there for the young ones and I can look back and see how things have changed. It's just a matter of letting people know what the community needs are. And most importantly, working together side-by-side, to achieve something so that in years to come you can say, 'Well I helped to do that,' or 'I made that happen.' Of course, things weren't always smooth. We had our ups and downs. But you've got to stand firm and speak your mind, things work out in the long run.

Then I got involved in taking the Djunagun Dance Troupe around to different places to perform. The boys got so good they started making their own dances up, creating their own things. One time in 1985 they even danced as a back-up with David Gulpilil down at Coffs Harbour. While the boys practised their dancing at the school during Aboriginal Studies the girls made jewellery. A lot of the boys that had already left school, they wanted to come back just so they could get into the Dance Troupe. We did so much at the schools with the kids. When we took the boys over to Kyogle to perform in their Fairymount Festival, the people were real pleased. It was something they had never seen before. But it was something for our boys too, because as they got out and danced among the crowds they got used to it. They said, 'Oh, this is good, eh, *I'm* not frightened. Are you shamed?' 'No, I'm not ashamed,' I said, 'You got nothing to be ashamed of. Just get in there and do the dances like you always to.' We did art at the school. They painted murals and the girls made beautiful jewellery. It was something that the kids could see what they did.

The Aboriginal community put out a lovely calender, Gungyah Ngallingnee—that means 'Listen to the People'. It's got photos of our community all the way through and beautiful Aboriginal poetry by Kath Walker. There's photos of the boys' art work and the Dance Troupe, jewellery-making and screenprinting. Oh! It's a nice calendar. The kiddies would look at it and say, 'Look, there's me, oh what!' They got real excited.

The kiddies have got to see something of themselves, what they've done and what they're about to do. That's the beauty part of it, when they can look at something they've done and say, 'By jove, I didn't know I could do that.' It's only just encouraging them and this is what we need today. Our young Aboriginal people, they only want a bit of encouragement. Not only the Aboriginal but the white children too. They've got to be encouraged because we've got to live together in Australia whether we like it or not. So there's no sense in squabbling with one another. This is what I can see starting to happen today, we're working together, achieving things together.

Now as I come back home to Maclean I can see there are a lot of things here they don't do that we did up at Tabulam. They haven't got a clue. I think that by getting around and communicating we'll be able to do these little things. It's only just working together and making things happen. I see Yamba and Maclean as tourist resorts. I think we should make the most of that. It's one way of sharing our ways to people we might not otherwise speak to. There could be boomerang-making and art work, more of the old ways. We could use the Aboriginal Totem. They might say, 'What you going to put with this?' Well I'd say, 'This is the emu. It's our totem.' Up there at Tabulam, it is all turtle. We call them *bingihn*.

See, there's two different kinds of turtle. The *mujang,* he lives in the swamp and he only crawls about on hot days, out on the grass or you'll see him when there's a flood. But the freshwater turtle, the *bingihn,* he's in the water all the time. The boys still go diving for turtle. By Jove we have a good feed, have a great big time. We'll just take some flour and baking powder, tea leaf and sugar, that's all we'd take. We spend the whole day on the river making damper and johnny cakes ready for the boys to come back with all these turtles.

They're already dead when the boys fetch them back so we open them up and put them in the fire.

Then it's time for sharing. We share them around with a bit of damper bread and it's lovely. That's what we do on the rivers up in Tabulam. These people down here, see they can't do what we do at Tabulam but they can get the oysters or the cobras and have a good old feed. To have a good feed of cobras, you go and look for the oak trees that have been in the water for some time. Open the tree up with an axe and hit it on the ground so that all the cobras come out. My, you can have a great feast on cobras! You can curry them or fry them. If you like, you can just simmer them in water. Bit of salt and pepper and damper bread, that would be our feed. Never go hungry. You can always find something in the bush to quell the hunger.

When we only ate the bush food our people were never sick. It's only lately we've been getting sick. One time we didn't know what diabetes was. Now it's killing a lot of our people. We had our own food. Even later on we made bread without the baking powder. We call it *munung*. That's from the Bundjalung, *munung*. A flat bread it is. We cook it many ways, either on the coals or in a frying pan or the best way is just on top of the fuel stove. To me it is all healthy.

If the kiddies get sores we teach the mothers how to bathe them and keep them clean. We rub olive oil all over the body. Olive oil is number one for everything. It's even good for colds. Every morning we would take a spoonful of oil. My daughter that's got the baby now, that's all she gives her baby. It keeps the cold off the chest or if he's got a cold it will bring all the phlegm right up. So there's a lot of things that are still good remedies today.

Didn't know what it was years ago to take aspirin or powders. They're doing more damage to your body than anything else. I remember my Mum, when she was sick she would take powders and more powders. Little did she know the damage they were doing. She thought the powders would kill the pains she had from her arthritis. The powders couldn't heal it because it was too far gone. You see, we can do a lot of harm to our bodies by taking the wrong kind of medicine. Sometimes I used to take powders just for the fun of it and you don't realise what it does to you till you start getting older. So we teach the mothers to rub the kiddies' backs with olive oil or camphorated oil.

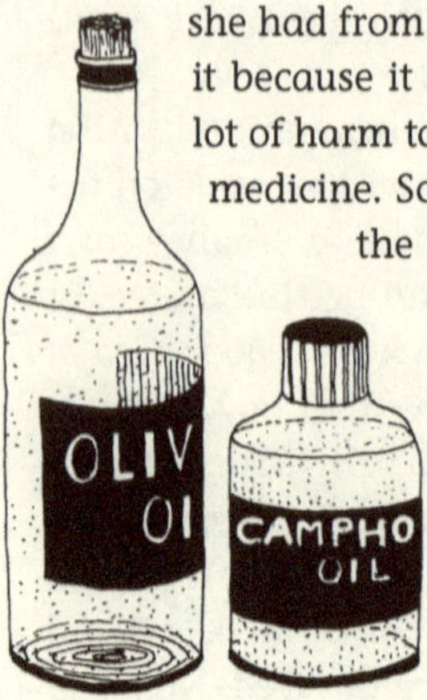

When our kids were sick we would make a big open fire in the living room and take their shirts off and sit them in front of the fire. Rub them back and front and under their arms. We'd massage their bodies all over. Next morning when they'd get up they were as good as gold, fit as a fiddle. You can't beat a good hand rub. Years ago the old people didn't have the oils you can get now. They just rubbed the fat of animals into their bodies. Goanna fat, they call it *ngamahl,* that's Bundjalung again. Even the porcupine fat, that's good for the body.

That's why when you see the Aboriginal people from way out, the ones who are still into their culture, they are so big and strong and healthy. We encourage the young mothers not to neglect their children and not to run them to the doctor every five minutes but to try some of the old treatments. They say, 'Aunty Della, that what you told me to do, it works.' As long as you massage your body, the bones and muscles can get so stiff and when you massage it you will feel beautiful within yourself.

Years ago on the island I remember a couple of boys were drowning. Dad swam out and brought them to shore. They were floating face down when he got to them. He lay them down on the wharf and began to suck from their mouths and massage their chests. Well now you give mouth-to-mouth but our people did that years and years ago. There were several boys that my Dad saved. Kiddies that would have been drowned, my Dad saved them.

There's a lot of things we can learn from our old people and there's so much you can do to help the people now. Young people are reaching out today and they want to find out more and more. Then again, we've got some ignorant people. Youngsters who don't want to know anything. They just want to go their own way. When you get sick is the time you've got all this tension and fear inside of you. Why? Because you worry. You've got to enjoy life today. As I say, God has given us the breath of life, the beautiful air that we can inhale, the freshness and beauty is all around us. If the doctor tells you something you worry, worry, worry. Yet there is still so much to learn from our old people, from the old ways.

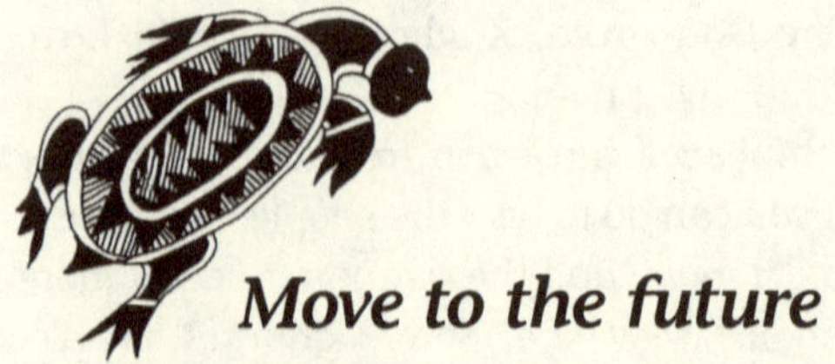

Move to the future

I've come back home now, to this beautiful place on the Clarence River called Maclean. As I sit down and think, my mind goes right back to when I was a child. All the things that have happened in my life, right through to the years I spent in Tabulam. I didn't even know that I was coming back here to live. There was a lot of sadness in leaving Tabulam, but I am here now to spend the rest of my days. I am glad that I've come back home to live.

When I came back I couldn't help but get involved with the schools. I go and talk to the children about different things. I talk about how I felt as a young Aboriginal girl and what it's like to be an older person now. Of course we talk a lot about the Aboriginal culture but you know, I didn't want to leave it there. I wanted to go on doing something more in the community. Every day I am doing things. I want to keep myself busy, keep my mind occupied in doing things for the community. I am a director for Yamboora, the Housing Co-operative that allocates houses to our people. I have applied to be a counsellor for the prison at Grafton. I am also the chairperson for Nungera Aboriginal Co-operative which was formed to help our people in housing, employment and things like that.

One day Val Close from the Lismore Technical and Further Education (TAFE) came over and set up workshops at the Hillcrest Mission here in Maclean. John Johnston from Grafton TAFE also came over and got involved. We do screenprinting, sewing, singing and a lot of other things too. We have a wonderful tutor there by the name of Bob Werry, young Bob, a very nice chap. I also teach Aboriginal Studies. We wrote a story about Ulgundahi Island and we talk about the dreamtime and all sorts of different things. This is all done at the community hall at Hillcrest. We get video tapes and look at different Aboriginal people from all parts of Australia. We can see what they are doing in their own areas and what they're on about. There's a lot of things that we are learning from this. I'm very pleased to be able to take part in these Aboriginal Studies which I think is a great thing for my people. Next year we hope to get more classes going through TAFE, God willing. I pray that God spares us to see another year through. This is something we can all look forward to. I know I'm looking forward to getting myself more involved.

Not long ago we made arrangements for about forty students and their teachers from Maclean High School to come out for one of our cooking days. We cooked damper and johnny cakes on the coals and also some lovely fresh fish. They tasted the different breads and they wanted more. This is the first time that the white kiddies down here have seen the cooking done like this and they just loved it. Of course, these days, to cook for a lot of people like that you really need a good gridiron. So, they made us up a big barbecue plate and we cooked lots of lovely gridiron cakes. You see, years ago we didn't have anything like that. We just cooked on the coals or in the ashes.

It was only recently that I had about twenty Year Seven high school kids who came out with their teacher. We had collected some cobras (wood worms) and it was the first time they had ever tasted cobra. Even the students and teacher thought they were nice, something different. You see, there's so much that the white people don't know about our culture, our lifestyle, our whole way of living. We're not a dirty lot of Aboriginal people. We are human beings. And we want to live and be happy with one another, on both sides. It's good that we can share like this, that they can come and learn from us and that we can learn from them. So you know what I mean, both sides have got a lot to give and a lot to receive. I think some people at times feel that because we've got a black skin we know nothing, but we can share with them. This is one way I know I can share something of the dreamtime that was told to me as a child. We can share some of it out and we can get them involved in learning our ways. This is what it's all about, living and sharing.

I want to work in the prisons as a counsellor. Unfortunately my health has stopped me going as much as I'd like to. I remember when I first went into the Grafton Gaol, it made me feel sick inside to see the young people. There was nothing really wrong with those boys but it made me feel no good inside. I was young myself once and I had plenty of brothers but the difference is that we weren't allowed to do the things that young people are doing today. This is the reason why there are more young people in gaol than older people, it's a shame.

I don't know really what we can do about the young people of today. I only hope that we can get them something to do. One idea would be to have a big property and have the younger ones who haven't got employment to work that property. Get somebody to be the caretaker sort of thing, to be the boss and organise the young ones. They could grow crops or have market gardens with vegetables and flowers. They could have an Aboriginal arts and craft shop where everybody in that community could contribute. That would give encouragement to other young Aboriginal people.

Look, we've got a lot of brainy boys and girls, but what else can they do but get up to mischief and mix with the wrong crowd. This is very sad because they've got no confidence in themselves. So we can help give them that confidence, make them feel important to the community. We need to create things for the young people of today. Let's face it, even though they've got the opportunity, some of them won't go on to get a full education. They only go to Year Nine or Ten, that's it, and they think they've got it all. What I'm saying is, that to get to the top where a white man is, you must learn and you must learn hard. As I look at the men in the gaol I feel sad. There's no future for them but coming out and doing the same thing again. What is there for the younger ones? What solution are we going to come up with?

It's hard because, then again, you see the ones who have got their certificates, qualifications for this or that, some of them can't get jobs. Where do you go from here? Let's ask ourselves that question. This is so important. Even when they get a better education they've still got to go to a bigger town to get the job anyhow. If they go to Sydney they've got to pay big rent. By the time the rent's paid, food and clothes are bought, the money's gone. How can they save? Unless they're making big money and to get the big money you've got to be a lawyer or barrister or something. It's sad when the young ones in the family have to leave home just to get a job.

With my church life going on, I find that I'd like to start something up here in Maclean. My people here, they do need the gospel. They need it badly I'd like to get a little hall for church so that we can all come together. We can send out invitations to sisters and brothers from all parts—from Sydney,

Moree, Taree, Inverell, Tabulam, Casino, Lismore, Grevillia and Kyogle. We've got sisters and brothers in the Lord from all over the place. We've got a lot of white brethren too that enjoy coming to our church. It's good to know that you've got white sisters and brothers.

Now today, I'm waiting to become a pastor I want to be somebody. I've always hoped and prayed that I could achieve something. This is my ambition in life, sharing and giving out God's word as a pastor. This is what I want to be I want to be there for my people. You know, sometimes when you lose a loved one, the minister doesn't know the person that he's giving the service for. When you have the service you're looking for that peace. It can be hard for the minister to know what to say. Sometimes I don't know myself what to say but we can only pass on the love and memories of that particular person who has died. Then you sing a song together with those that have lost a loved one. This is what it's all about. Aboriginal people sharing with Aboriginal people, living together and looking for that hope. The hope that is within Jesus Christ our Lord.

I've met some nice ministers down here and over at Grafton. We all had this meeting with one another and it filled my heart with joy just to know that there were ministers reaching out, who want to find out more about our ways. We had a seminar at Grafton and it truly was a sharing time. They questioned me and to the best of my ability I answered them. I felt lovely.

Now that I'm chairperson for the Nungera Aboriginal Cooperative I feel good, for lots of reasons but most of all it's getting to know the people and what they're all about. It makes us feel that we're somebody in the community. We can talk things over and see all the good that can come from sitting down and talking things through. I used to go up to work every day but now I've got these sore feet. They've slowed me down a lot which is probably a good thing. If you push yourself too hard, well then, you're no good to anybody.

I'd like to see something happen in Yamba for my people. There's plenty that could be done both in and out of the town for the Aboriginal and white communities alike. Every time I drive past the big water reservoir I can visualise in my mind how it could be painted. Oh, it takes my eyes every time. Black and white could paint a big mural on it for everyone to see. They could work together side-by-side, sharing and caring.

Sometimes you hear people say, 'Oh, the Aboriginal people have got it good. They've got all this free money coming in.' That's not true. We still pay tax and this is our land. We pay tax money for own land. It's not only the white man who pays. Today we are more equal, although we have a black skin. I'm not going to let myself be put down just because I have a black skin. I am what I am!

I love to talk about doing different things in the community. These days at home I make Aboriginal jewellery out of porcupine quills and beads. So you see, there's always something you can find to do. Self-esteem, confidence in oneself, you know what I mean. I am not really on handouts. I don't feel I am. It's not only the Aboriginal people who are struggling to survive. There's a lot of other people as well. I go into St Vincent de Paul, I sometimes go in for a bit of a stickybeak and I see a lot of white people in there. They need to go there too. It's no shame. That's what the St Vincent de Paul is there for, to help people. Not to grab money off the people but to help them. I know because I lived near Casino for many years. I have some lovely friends over at Casino, the likes of Mrs Cahill. She was a caretaker for St Vincent de Paul. All the ladies in there are very lovely people. Still today I go in to see them. We have a talk and a bit of a laugh cause they're my friends and I'm their friend. It's good when you can sit down and talk to others.

As Aboriginal people we can always laugh at things, even when we've got nothing. We can spin one another yarns. Not worry about anything but just sit down and have a good laugh. Even today, my sisters and I still sit down and talk about the things we used to do as kids. We go right back and now that we're older we can laugh at the things we got up to. Of course, we say we wouldn't do things like that today.

It brings to mind my own kids. As a mother myself I sometimes get very lonely because I've got no-one here with me at the moment. All my kids have gone. Every now and then they take a trip to come home to see me, to give me a surprise. They stay a night or two and away they go again. When my children were small we were all the time sharing with one another. You didn't really have time to get lonely.

I've got one fellow down here playing football at Maclean. He's the one I said played for the Canberra Raiders. He also played for Sydney with the Rabbitohs. That's the one named Billy Walker. He has a game of golf too, now and again. He's good at the golf. Another son, Rocky, is one of the top players for the Grafton Ghosts. My other sons play league for teams in the Upper Clarence. Two of my boys are working at the moment, building new roads and homes on the mission at Tabulam. Cedric has a good job at the big hospital in Toowoomba. Bella was the teachers' aide at Tabulam School until she left to start a family of her own. Little Della did some modelling for a while here in Maclean and now she is working in Sydney. So I'm pleased that my children have grown up to do me proud.

With a family of fourteen I have many grandchildren—twenty all together. I have eight granddaughters and twelve grandsons. When they come home to see me I suppose they're so happy to be down here with their grandmother, they think in their little hearts and minds that they can just run wild. I'm a very strict grandmother but I love them and I care for them. Before they go to bed at night I tell them stories. Some of them are from the dreamtime and some we read out of books.

There are lots of other kiddies who look on me as a grandmother. Over the years I have fostered many children, even white kiddies at times. There's that many of them and I love them all I suppose it's just the Aboriginal way. They all call me Ma Walker, even the adults. When I lived in Bonalbo different children would come to my home after school. They ate what my children ate. Whatever I had in the cupboard they would eat. Now when I cook a feed, I make a big pot so that if there are any extra people in my home we can sit down and share the meal together.

I'm getting on in years now. It's my turn to sit back and watch the young ones grow. As they grow from little babies through to their teenage years, I see the need for them to learn more of the old ways. The old ways were all about giving and sharing. What the younger generation do today is totally different to my days. It's up to us oldies to guide our young ones through their growing years. We must teach them to care and to share. So for our children's sake and their children too, let's live together. Share the beauty that we have in this lovely country. There's enough room for all of us to live and share together. We've got the beauty and the love to give to one another—me and you together.

PLATE 1. *Lilly Cameron (Della's aunty), Milar Laurie (Della's aunty), Bella Cameron (Della's mother) and Elsie Creag in an Ulgundahi Island School photograph, c. 1910. Photograph courtesy of Mrs K Bolton.*

PLATE 2. Della's sister Margaret, in the middle of the back row, outside the Ulgundahi Sunday School, c. 1937. Photograph courtesy of the Maclean Historical Society.

PLATE 3. Della's father Rocky Laurie, from a photograph of the Harwood Football Club team, 1925.

PLATE 4. Cane cutters on Ulgundahi Island. Photograph courtesy of Brenda Smith.

PLATE 5. Della's sister's house Ulgundahi Island during the 1956 floods. Photograph courtesy of Brenda Smith.

PLATE 6. Pippi Beach in front of Pippi Beach Mission, Yamba, 1988. Photograph by Caroline Pascoe.

PLATE 7. Craigmore Guest House, Yamba, 1940s. Photograph courtesy of the Yamba Historical Society.

PLATE 8. *Della and William Walker at home, Bonalbo, 1969.*

PLATE 9. Tabulam junior football players, 1950s, with Lenny at the bottom on the left and John (Dooster) on the bottom right. Photograph courtesy of Austin Soorley.

PLATE 10. *William Walker at Rio, Tabulam, 1958.*

PLATE 11. *William Walker with some of his children at home, Bonalbo, 1969. Photograph courtesy of Susan Donnelly.*

PLATE 12. Della and her sons, Bonalbo, 1972.

PLATE 13. A baptism held at Rocky River, with Della at the bottom right, 1960.

PLATE 14. *Della and her sister Ester, with an original silk screenprint, taken at Hillcrest Aboriginal Village, Maclean, 1988.*

PLATE 15. *Della junior with some jewellery made at Tabulam, 1985. Photograph by Caroline Pascoe*

PLATE 16. *Lewis Walker with one of his 'traditional' paintings. Photograph courtesy of Tryphena McShane.*

PLATE 17. *Lewis Walker playing a didjeridu with the Djunagun Dance Troupe, Grafton, 1985. Photograph by Tryphena McShane.*

PLATE 18. The Djunagun Dance Troupe poster surrounded by photos of the boys in the troupe. Photograph by Tryphena McShane.

PLATE 19. *Rocky Walker of the Grafton Ghosts tackling Billy Walker of the Lower Clarence in a match played at Maclean, 1987. Photograph courtesy of the* Daily Examiner.

PLATE 20. *Della Walker, Yamba, 1988. Photograph by Caroline Pascoe.*

www.ingramcontent.com/pod-product-compliance
Lightning Source LLC
LaVergne TN
LVHW051008080826
845145LV00009B/2515

* 9 7 8 0 8 5 5 7 5 2 1 2 5 *